Experience the Power of God's Presence

A Call to intimacy with God

HARRY MUYENZA

Exson Publishing

Table of Contents

Acknowledgements
Preface

◇◇◇

Experience the Power of God's Presence: A Call to intimacy with God.

Copyright © 2012 Harry Muyenza by Exson Publishing

For more information contact:

Exson Publishing
a member of Exson Corporate Solutions LLC
Telephone: 1-574-643 1113
Fax: 1-574 307 1285
Toll Free: 1 877 885 6297
Email: *harryexson@hotmail.com*
www.harrymuyenza.com
www.exsonpublishing.com
www.worldimpactforchrist.org

SPECIAL THANKS

There are many people, too numerous to write how much each one of you means to me and how your contributions, mentorship, inspiration and support have been so valuable and have greatly influenced my life and ministry in a big way. My special thanks should go to the following people:

My beloved wife, Budile my sweetheart, you have always been so supportive and you have helped me grow and enhance my insight into the things of God. I am deeply grateful and will always be indebted to you, honey. My dear sons, Theo and Ti, you are so wonderful! I appreciate you allowing me the time as I worked on this project.

Apostle Dr. Stanley Ndovie, you have been such a great mentor and inspiration to me. You have been a father.

Dr Jaspine Bilima, thank you for your support. You have inspired me greatly as I stepped out to work on this book.

Mrs. Phyllis Wiseman, thank you for all your help and pointers as I put the manuscript together. I appreciate your technical insights, encouragement and support.

Pastor Chris Daza, I thank God for you .You are one of the few men that impacted my life in the area of worship.

Pastor Moffat Mtegha, Pastor Isaac Mkukupa, thank you for believing in me. I will always be grateful for your support and encouragement in the worship ministry.

◇◇◇

A WORD TO MY DEAR READER

You thought that it was you who was waiting on God, yet, it is God who has been waiting on you all along. He has been waiting for you to hunger for Him. God has promised to satisfy and fill those who are hungry and thirsty. I believe this is the major qualification for one to experience the supernatural presence of God. The Holy Spirit is still here on Earth with us; He has not returned to the Father in heaven, this guarantees us that we can experience the blessing which comes from the presence of God. You will be infused with His power and glory we so desperately need in these last days. I hope and pray you will be the candidate for God's filling and satisfaction.

Let us begin our journey from here right away, as we seek to enter into His presence to be empowered and ignited with a longing for that intimate relationship with our God through worship.

May God richly bless you as you take time to read this book.

Harry E. Muyenza

INTRODUCTION

Do you want to be blessed? Do you desire to have an intimate, empowering relationship that is so deep and personal? Having served in the music ministry for a number of years, there are things I have learned, observed and experienced concerning the subject of praise and worship. Therefore, I feel prompted by the Holy Spirit to share some of these things through this book to as many people as the Lord would allow me.

Everyone desires to be blessed of the Lord. There is a blessing from the Lord for everybody. You are the right candidate for God's blessing. You can be empowered to be blessed and succeed. To be empowered simply means to be given power or authority and it also means to be given a sense of confidence or self-esteem. Thus, the power of His presence will vitalize us, give us new energy: an opportunity to be powered up again in order to fulfill God's purpose for our lives.

Therefore, "experience the power of his presence- a call to intimacy with God" is meant to ignite your passion for more of God's presence where you can derive the power to prosper and be all that you were meant to be. It is here to propel you to a place where you can hunger and thirst after God more than ever before and be drawn into the Lord's presence. We can have an intimate relationship with God right here on Earth; I am not talking about when we get to heaven someday, but right here, here on Earth in our time. In this book we will highlight on some things that happen when we open ourselves to the Lord in worship to God.

The power of God's presence is released when we make ourselves available in His presence t praise and worship. I am intensely aware that at times it is almost impracticable to worship the Lord in the midst of adversity and difficulties. When things do not seem to work the way we would like to see, I endeavor to encourage you to step out in faith and express your praise without reservation no matter the circumstances. Yet you can learn to praise and worship the Lord in the midst of your difficulties and summon the blessing which descends from the heavenly storehouse upon us His people when we draw into His presence.

You can choose to give God the before it happens praise. You can begin to praise Him for that blessing, for that victory, for that promotion even before it manifests in the Earthly-physical realm from the supernatural realm- the realm of the Spirit. Your blessing will surely come, but it must be called from the spiritual realm first. Worship therefore, is one way you can call your blessings.

In a world full of problems and catastrophes it has become so easy to get distracted and lose focus. My earnest desire is that the information contained in this book will bring about a hunger and thirst for more of God- a longing for His presence. I trust God for a rekindling of the passion for the Lord; the zeal for the house of the Lord will consume the church again. I know as we draw closer and closer to the end of times things will get worse and will never get any better in this world. But it will not be so for the body of Christ, because Christ is coming for a vibrant, strong and glorious church, a bride adorned ready for the marriage supper of the lamb.

I believe the church will only come up to this level once it takes its rightful position before the Lord in worship. It is only then that His power will be her portion. It is at this time that His power will overflow; supernatural manifestation of God's power will ensue. The church will be empowered to succeed as she responds to this call to an intimacy with God.

◇◇◇

PART 1 - UNDERSTANDING PRAISE & WORSHIP

◇◇◇

CHAPTER 1

WHAT IS WORSHIP?

We have defined worship nominally as a time we attend our regular church meetings in the traditional church setting. Worship is usually associated with church gathering mainly on a specific day of the week set aside by our particular denomination as a day of worship. These special days of worship are generally, a Friday, Saturday or Sunday for most people.

Under denominational setting, we have a set out program and protocol, which are largely observed as the mode of operation. This might include the outward expression like walking in a holy manner and holding of the Bible close to the chest to show a state of piety. We may even do the cross markings, a bowing as we pass by the altar or pulpit as a sign of reverence, which is usually exaggerated and is not reflective of the genuineness of our commitment to God.

Commonly such practices have an inherent capacity of deception and place the people which practice them under a sense of false humility. This eventually indoctrinates the people to a great deal that such practices are woven in a tricky manner becoming the core fabric of their belief system.

How do we define worship?

In a simple definition worship is explained as the disposition with an attitude that is inclined towards paying homage to a higher power. It is a state of being where a lesser being gravitates towards a perceived higher being. Worship means adoration, reverence, devotion, love and respect to a deity. This deity is considered a holy being, a divine being and is generally, considered as a superior being. This is done as a means of honor or reverence which we call worship

13

What is the origin of worship?

All forms and manner of worship have their own distinct origins. Man has a part within him which is always reaching out for a supernatural experience. This part of man is always longing for an encounter with a greater power, usually a deity. God Himself has placed this in us, but it has been diverted by Satan to lead people into various forms of perversions and deceptions. Man has, in many cases, fallen prey to seducing and deceiving demons which have subtly led him into false religion and worshipping of things which are not to be worshipped. This has also culminated from a deep desire for power, control, peace, riches and wealth. Man is always looking out for knowledge, guidance, and enlightenment. His fascination and insecurity about the future has led him to seek a supernatural experience. He tries to tap into what the future holds by contacting the spiritual realm, usually through some form of worship.

Humanity has fallen prey to deception

As a consequence of this hollow in man which is always seeking out to acquire some supernatural encounter or knowledge about what the future holds has, consequently, made himself vulnerable to seducing spirits.

One of the signs of the last days or the end of the age is deception. People will not endure sound doctrine. Seducing spirits from the devil will increasingly arise to lead people astray through various forms of deception. Many will give in to false teachings and doctrines, which are in opposition with biblical truth. Jesus revealed this to His disciples in responding to their question concerning what the signs of His coming shall be in the book of Matthew 24:24 "For there shall arise false Christs, and false prophets, and shall show great signs and wonders; insomuch that, if it were possible, they shall deceive the very elect".

Jesus said do not be deceived for many false prophets will arise in those days. The apostle Paul also spoke and confirms this fact in some of his letters such as his letter to Timothy.

"Now the Spirit speaketh expressly, that in the latter times some shall depart from the faith, giving heed to seducing spirits and doctrines of devils" ~(1Timothy 4: 1).

Understand that these false prophets shall teach and propagate false doctrines and teachings of demons. So they will deceive many, especially those believers which are always seeking out for miracles or some form of revelation. These false teachers will possess some demonic powers to perform some miracles too. Remember in Egypt when Moses was sent by God to free the children of Israel from slavery. When Moses performed the first miracle, turning his rod into a serpent, Pharaoh's magicians produced theirs too. The difference was that Moses' serpent swallowed up the counterfeits of the magicians. Therefore, I believe when these false prophets and teachers appear in these last days, performing their demonic miracles, at the same time, there shall be an acceleration of outstanding genuine miracles in the body of Christ which will supersede the demonic ones. This is when the greater miracle will take place. These are the miracles of which Jesus spoke about saying:

"Verily, verily, I say unto you, He that believeth on me, the works that I do shall he do also, and greater works than these shall he do; because I go unto my Father ~ (John 14:12).

Therefore, this calls for wisdom and discernment for believers not to be deceived. Those who are properly grounded in the word of truth shall be able to discern the false. They will discern the genuine from the counterfeit by testing the spirits.

"Beloved, believe not every spirit, but try the spirits whether They are of God: because many false prophets are gone out into the world" ~(1 John 4:1).

The believers should be prudent, and diligently examine the scriptures in order to tell and expose the false teachings like the early Christians in Berea did in the book of Acts 17: 11. It is reported about them, "These were nobler than those in Thessalonica, in that they received the word with all readiness of mind, and searched the Scriptures daily, whether those things were so". You should not just accept any doctrine at its face value. You should carefully validate the messages presented to you on the basis of God's written word, the Bible.

Let me go back to this spirit of deception that is facing us. Man has now fallen prey and has subjected himself to the spirit of deception. He has been subtly enticed into demonic activities without himself knowing it. Man has ended up getting involved consciously or unconsciously in sorcery, witchcraft, Satanism, Freemasonry, and Islam. These are some of the elusive false religions people are trapped in as a result. Many others are involved in the Eastern Philosophy, Secret Society, Rainbow Girls, the Shiners, DeMolay and many others. There are so many other religions and cults which even counterfeit Christianity such as the Jehovah's Witness and the Church of Jesus Christ of the Latter Day Saints (LDS) also known as the Mormon Church. Suffice to say all of them originate from some form of superstition and occult, which is all satanic in nature. I will reserve my exposé of the many other false religions operating out there for purposes of maintaining our focus on the subject matter for this book. However, it is vitally important for me to point out their main features or characteristics, which will help you in identifying them. You will discover that all false cults share most of these features:

They all deny the deity of Jesus Christ as only Savior or Messiah, or God and Son of God. They declare and profess Jesus as merely a good teacher or one of the great prophets of old.

They teach that human works and effort must earn salvation.

They do not believe in the trinity of God- the father, Son and the Holy Spirit.

They teach that man is god in himself and that he can ultimately, become God and therefore, man has no need for God.

They all claim to lead people into the true light and discovery of self.

They teach that man can gain some form of power to control his own affairs, other people, obtain luck and a promise of a secure financial freedom and wealthy life.

Their operations are normally secretive and restricted to a specific chosen few that have passed through some special ritual or rites of initiation.

Their followers are usually sworn into an oath of secrecy about what takes place in their places of worship or temples. Disclosure is usually punishable severely- such punishment may include physical harm even death.

They claim and teach that they possess knowledge that is mysteriously restricted to only the initiated ones.

They believe in the plurality of God, some clearly practice worship of idols and fellow human beings who are usually founders of such faiths usually called prophets.

They deceive people into believing that you can pray, sacrifice, or be baptized on behalf of or for a dead beloved one who died a sinner so they can be translated or transferred from hell or purgatory to Heaven.

Let me emphatically state in no uncertain terms that these are deceptions from the devil. Now having barely scratched on the surface about these false religions, the occult and their lead identities, it is imperative that we establish who our genuine and true object of worship really is.

◇◇◇

CHAPTER 2

WHO MUST WE WORSHIP?

Man is a created being and God is the Superior or higher being. That is why our study is focused and directed at getting us to a place where we can effectively worship God—The God who made the heavens and the Earth and the entire universe. His name is Jehovah, the God and Father of our Lord Jesus Christ, the only true living God in the entire universe, the God who is omnipresent, omnipotent and omniscient- ever present everywhere at the same time, all knowing, and all powerful God. He is the uncreated eternal God. The triune God, ordinarily called God in trinity, that is God the Father, God the Son and God the Holy Spirit. He is the only creator of all things.

This is the God we must all worship. He is the one we must encounter and experience. He is such a great, loving, and merciful God. However, He exercises His authority over all with truth and justice. His judgments are true and righteous. It is He whom we must worship—He is the exclusive object of all worship. No human being or any man-made image or any of God's creation is to be worshipped or paid homage. When man turns away from worshipping God, His creator, he ends up worshipping the created things. Therefore, man loses his position as God's delegated authority in the Earth (Genesis 1: 26).

As a superior being man degrades himself by worshipping such created beings such as his fellow man, animals like in other religions, especially those in the East, like Hindu where they have over a million gods. People worship things that are part of God's creation. These things are never to be placed in a position of deity to be worshipped and adored.

Some worship these gods in ignorance and tradition having been indoctrinated from their childhood. Sadly, most children are initiated into such false worship in their time of absolute innocence as babies against their will and volition. They are subjected to worshipping of gods whom they have no personal understanding or knowledge of. When they grow up, such people cannot explain who the god they serve is, because there is no intimate, personal relationship. When you ask them all they will tell you is that they inherited the religion: our forefathers passed it down to us, and so we grew up in it. Such religions have robbed people of their God-given freewill. They are not free agents - they cannot freely exercise their own choice and discretion in following and belonging to such faiths. In short, they worship a god who has been forced or imposed on them, and they have grown and learned to accept and embrace as their own god.

One thing I love about the God of our Lord Jesus Christ is that He does not force himself on us, but He allows us to use our brain and willpower to either follow Him or not. This is so evident throughout the Bible. For instance, when God created the first human beings Adam and Eve, placing them in the Garden of Eden, they were given the freedom of choice. He did not control them, but gave them the liberty to exercise their own freewill. He equipped them with all the knowledge of His will. He made known to them that the consequences of disobedience would result in death while their obedience and adherence to His law would guarantee them eternal life. He warned them that "in the day you shall eat of the forbidden fruit you shall surely die".

"And the LORD God commanded the man, saying, of every tree of the garden thou mayest freely eat: But of the tree of the knowledge of good and evil, thou shalt not eat of it: for in the day that thou eatest thereof thou shalt surely die" ~(Genesis 2:16-17).

At the same time, he told them they were free to eat of any tree in the garden including the tree of life, which had they eaten from it, they were going to enjoy eternal life with unlimited access and continued fellowship with God their creator. This is the kind of God who is always reaching out to us; He would love to have a more personal relationship with us. It is Him we all must worship.

How do we worship?

To avoid being led into falsehood and error we must first establish right here how we can worship God. Others will tell you it does not matter what medium you use to worship, how, when or where you worship. This is dangerous as it can make us vulnerable to demons.

On the outset, we need to know that God can only be worshipped through one - that is through Jesus Christ the Son of the Living God. He is the only way to the Father.

"Jesus saith unto him, I am the way, the truth and the life: no man cometh unto the Father, but by me" ~(John 14:6)

If we dare to reach God in our worship through some other personality we will end up getting lost. Jesus is the only door to the Father. "I am the door: by me if any man enters in, he shall be saved, and shall go in and out and find pasture" ~(John 10:9).

When we try to enter in through some other door we indeed end up in the realm of the supernatural. Unfortunately, we end up in a wrong place altogether, because all other doors will lead to the supernatural realm of the Satan. However, when we enter in through the door of Jesus Christ, we enter the supernatural realm of God.

Therefore, our primary way to get our access into the presence of God is going through Jesus Christ. Our worship must culminate from our personal relationship with God through Jesus Christ His Son, "for through him we both have access by one Spirit unto the Father" ~(Ephesians 2:18). Thus, we have a direct access to the Father through Jesus Christ, the Son of the living God, who is the only mediator between all humanity and God. "For There is one God, and one mediator between God and men, the man Christ Jesus"~(1Timothy 2:5).

You will understand that false religion is anything which does not stand for the true religion. It is in reality a counterfeit or something literally strange or bogus, forged, and fake. These are mostly contradictory to each other. Every false religion is in opposition to the truth of God and His word. Let me dare to give you a very brief, easy and straightforward definition of falsehood or false religion according to the Holy Scriptures, the Bible. I emphasize on this, because these false religions use some counterfeit forms of books which may contain small positions of twisted, quotation from the true book of God and these portions of the Bible are usually quoted out of context: "I have not written unto you, because ye know not the truth, but because ye know it, and that no lie is of the truth" ~ (1 John 2:21).

Any religion, no matter its name, which does not acknowledge Jesus Christ as Savior and Lord, is no question of the devil— it is there only to serve satanic purposes.

"Who is a liar but he that denieth that Jesus is, the Christ? He is antichrist that denieth the Father and the Son. Whosoever denieth the Son, the same hath not the Father: but he that acknowledgeth the Son hath the Father also" ~(1 John 2:22-23).

They can call God with different names, but if they do not embrace Jesus Christ as the Son of God and the only Savior or Messiah of the whole world, then you know their claim of sharing or worshipping a one and same God with you is empty and false. They are definitely worshipping a different God. The Bible unapologetically calls them Anti-Christ- meaning they are against Jesus Christ. Whoever is not with us is against us! Now here's the amazing thing about real Christianity- we do not pick up guns or bombs ~(we do not embrace the barbaric ideology of hate, where we become suicide bombers) to kill those who differ with our theology or religious ideology. They may even call us infidels or rebels, but as Christians, we pick up love and share the love of Jesus Christ with them in spite of our differences in theology or position of belief.

These are the religions that may acknowledge Jesus only as a prophet, but deny His deity as God. They deny the very truth that Jesus was God and at the same time man. They may call Him a good-teacher or one of the great prophets. This is all done in a bid to confuse and entice you into believing that you share the same God with them when the opposite is true. It is a clear-cut lie from the pit of hell. This is the very lie from the devil. Satan knows the best way to deceive someone is to wrap a lie with half-truth in it. That is the natural tactic of the devil. If you belong to such a cult or religion you will be insane to continue, having been given this truth.

Dear reader, you know as you read where you belong. It is never too late for you to change over to the true God. You can find this true God, through Jesus Christ. I am not talking about joining a particular church or religion. This is not about joining religion. The church by itself cannot save you. Religion is merely man's search for God, but Christianity is beyond religion. It is coming to a personal, living and loving relationship with your creator through Jesus Christ the Son of God. You are not holding this booklet by accident. Even if it were, it would still be a good accident. Why do I call it such? Because this accident will not endanger or kill you, rather it will draw you unto salvation and give you a new hope for the future through the person of Jesus Christ. This is no mere coincidence, but a divine set-up. It is a God-incidence thing, because He loves and cares so much about you. He loves you so much that He had to take upon himself man's form, wearing a human body in order to reach out to you. He left His mighty throne and glory coming to Earth in order to save us. He is so passionate about you, that even the angels in heaven are amazed and wonder why man is so dear to God's heart, such that one testified in a certain place saying, "What is man, that thou art mindful of him? Or the son of man, that thou visitest him?"~(Hebrews 2:6; Psalms 8:4-5).

God cares for you so much so that He was willing to offer Himself as a sacrifice, died on the cross so that you do not have to die and go to hell. He wants above everything else for you to spend eternity with Him in heaven.

We share the amazing grace and love of God that is found in Jesus Christ. There is no greater love than this, that while we were yet, sinners Christ loved us so much that He died for us on the cross. The righteous one died for the unrighteous and the innocent was condemned to death for the guilty. He shed His blood to redeem us and cleanse us from all sin. The righteous man who knew no sin, whom even Pontius Pilate testified, saith unto them, "Behold, I bring him forth to you that ye may know that I find no fault in him" referring to Jesus Christ~(John 19:4).

While there may be no specific positioning in worship it is important that we know that we can worship anywhere, anytime and in the manner that is acceptable to God. For example, you can worship God facing any direction, "Jesus saith unto her, Woman, believe me, the hour cometh, when ye shall neither in this mountain, nor yet, at Jerusalem, worships the Father"~(John 4:21).

However, at the same time you cannot be directed as a general rule or religious statute by your religion to worship

God in certain places like under the water, in trees, mountain, in the air except while traveling by airplane or meeting for worship only late at night. This is undoubtedly very questionable. I am talking about those religions that only meet during late night hours from between 12 midnight to 4 am.

Expressive worship - Going beyond the veil

I have seen that most of the worship is depicted by the outward expressions. Nevertheless, worship should transcend the mere outward expressions even though these are significantly an integral part of it. Our worship of God must be in the company of both the outward as well, as the innermost part of our being. In actual fact these outward expressions must communicate the deep feelings from our inner man, deep self, who is called the Spirit man. Knowing that man is a triune being; that is the real person is the spirit who has a soul and he resides in a human flesh we call the body.

"And the very god of peace sanctify you wholly; and I pray god your whole spirit and soul and body be preserved blameless unto the coming of our lord Jesus Christ" ~(1 Thessalonians 5:23)..

This is no surprise to me that each time our flesh is inflicted with pain, we usually say, "oh my arm hurts, or my head or toe hurts really badly." The real you is the one who claims ownership in these instances, pointing to the location of the pain been felt at that particular part of the body.

Therefore, worship must involve our total humanity. David said, in the book of Psalms 103:1 "Bless the LORD, O my soul: and all that is within me bless His holy name"

This suggests to us that worship may arguably involve some or all of our being. Our worship should engage our

25

whole being, spirit, soul and body, "Jesus said unto him, Thou shalt love the Lord thy God with all thy heart, and with all thy soul, and with thy entire mind"~(Matthew 22:37).

Worship transcends mere reading of songs or hymns from a book routinely when we meet in our respective congregations. We will devote a great deal of our concentration on this aspect of worship later in this study as we look at elements which constitute worship- which is pleasing to God. This is the worship that will bring us into contact with the supernatural presence of our creator. The presence of God comes by the Holy Spirit, who works to manifest the power of God. It is Him who empowers us to effectively serve Him. If we can find our way and the right approach into the presence of God, we can then meet the person of the Holy Ghost, who empowers and energizes us.

"But ye shall receive power, after that the Holy Ghost is come upon you: and ye shall be witnesses unto me both in Jerusalem, and in all Judea, and in Samaria, and unto the uttermost part of the Earth" ~ (Acts 1:8).

This is the power that will cause us to be transformed into a breed of people who will influence the course of history and draw people to a personal experience of God.

This power is so dynamic that it knows no sinner who cannot be radically changed into a saint, it knows no poor person who cannot be made rich, and it knows no sickness it cannot heal.

◇◇◇

26

CHAPTER 3

WHY SHOULD WE WORSHIP?

I remember being born in a so-called Christian family, where I was taught from a very tender age that we were Christian of the Church of Central Africa Presbyterian (CCAP). I was devoted to the church, attending Sunday school, all the way through the classes. I got baptized and was acknowledged as a Christian, but yet just following the crowd without having a more personal relationship with the Lord. Thank God, who is rich in mercy for His grace that I heard the gospel and decided to believe in Jesus Christ-repenting of all my sins and becoming a born again Christian having understood the love and grace of God, which brings men unto salvation through faith in Jesus Christ.

Pursuant to experiencing God's love, kindness and mercy we overflow with gratitude and worship to Him. The love of God became so real to me from then on. I understood the meaning of the death of Jesus Christ on the cross. A passionate love for the Lord began in my life. I wanted to do whatever He wanted me to do. All I wanted was to be with the Lord in Heaven. I wanted to live a life that was pleasing to the Lord. I wanted just to spend time in prayer and worship before the Lord.

In response to His love for us

We need to move away from that mechanical type of worship, where we worship as by duty. But our worship must be a response to the love and the grace of God. We were once not a people of God, but now we are His chosen people. We who were far away from the grace of God have now been brought into His Kingdom and have been made His children by faith in Jesus Christ. Even though we may not see so many reasons for worshipping God, but the salvation of lives is the greatest reason to worship Him. You see we were destined for hell, eternal separation from God, but by His grace, He has had mercy upon us. The Bible says, "But God commendeth His love toward us, in that, while we were yet sinners, Christ died for us"~(Romans 5:8). It is not a result of our works of righteousness, but His love and grace, which have drawn us nigh to Him. We did not merit this salvation: "For it is by grace you have been saved, through faith—and this is not from yourselves, it is the gift of God—not by works, so that no one can boast" ~ (Ephesians 2:8–9).

Christ paid a price on our behalf. We did not do anything good to deserve such a great sacrifice of the righteous for the unrighteous, but out of His goodness, we have received His mercy, love and forgiveness. We have done nothing to earn such great love and mercy.

"For he hath made him to be sin for us, who knew no sin; that we might be made the righteousness of God in him" ~ (2 Corinthians 5:21).

The love of God has now won our hearts, love and trust so that our natural response is to thank, praise, and worship Him. His love for us has birthed a deep love for Him in us. We must allow the love of God to win our hearts first, and then it is easy to worship Him out of love and grateful heart - not duty or fear. There is no fear in love, for perfect love casts out fear. We do not worship God out of a heart of fear or compulsion, but from a willing heart —where liberal offering of worship springs forth. Our worship then ceases to be merely mechanical, but becomes natural and heart to heart as we respond to God's love. We allow our hearts to be consumed with the love of God knowing that he loves us so much with an unfailing love. He is so much in love with us even when we are far away from Him. He loves us even when we are unfaithful, when we have messed up and

28

fallen short of His expectation. Realize that he is ever reaching-out with hands open-wide to take us back in even we stumble and fall. It is significantly invigorating to know that He loves us for who we are and not what we have done. There is nothing that we have done that will make him close the door. Nothing that we have ever done will change His love for us. He loves us in spite of what we have done. There is nothing you could do to make him love you more, because He loves us with an everlasting and immeasurable love. Consequently, we passionately reciprocate that love through worship.

Different ways of worship

People have defined their own way of how to worship. Some believe in worshipping facing a particular direction, dressed in a particular manner and doing it in a certain fashion. The Bible has a few instances where worship was directly defined in relation to direction but suffice to say that this was very situational to the circumstances which were prevalent at the time. The Bible also reveals to us how people worshipped God in the Old Testament days, especially the children of Israel. It is only right and proper to learn how to worship God from the people of the Bible. It is because we were a people without God in the world, we were far away, but God in His mercy has now reconciled us to Himself. He has adopted us into His family and made us His own, placing us in the royal priesthood status,

"But ye are a chosen generation, a royal priesthood, a holy nation, a peculiar people; that ye should show forth the praises of him who hath called you out of darkness into his marvelous light"~(1Peter 2:9).

"Which in time past were not a people, but are now the people of God: which had not obtained mercy, but now have obtained mercy" ~(1Peter 2:10).

If you are a gentile, you were outside the commonwealth of Israel, but now we have been made partakers of that divine nature, with all the rights and benefits through Christ Jesus;

"That at that time ye were without Christ, being aliens from the commonwealth of Israel, and strangers from the covenants of promise, having no hope, and without God in the world. But now in Christ Jesus ye who sometimes were, far off are made nigh by the blood of Christ" ~(Ephesians 2:12-13).

"Now therefore, ye are no more strangers and foreigners, but fellow citizens with the saints, and of the household of God" ~(Ephesians 2:19).

For example, while Daniel and his friend were in captivity in Babylon, they would pray and worship facing Jerusalem:

"Now when Daniel knew that the writing was signed, he went into his house; and his windows being open in his chamber toward Jerusalem, he kneeled upon his knees three times a day, and prayed, and gave thanks before his God, as he did formerly" ~(Daniel 6:10).

In the New Testament we also see Jesus and His disciples would often, go out into the mountain to pray, they would usually fall down and pray. "And he (meaning Jesus) went a little farther, and fell on his face, and prayed, saying, O my Father, if it be possible, let this cup pass from me: nevertheless not as I will, but as thou wilt" ~(Matthew 26:39).

David had his own way of worshipping the Lord which may be of particular interest to us as we continue to look at a few things concerning praise and worship. He is the one who through the inspiration of the Holy Spirit, authored most of passages in the book of Psalms. I believe the book of Psalms s is so valuable when it comes to worshipping. Here are some of ways worship is depicted in the Bible: -

We worship the Lord with dancing:
One can praise God with dancing and singing. There are so many styles of dance depending on where one comes from and based on cultural heritage. Usually, the uniqueness of a people is reflected in the way they express themselves through singing and dancing. Hence you can praise God with the dance as long as it is not sexually provocative or seductive. Pay attention to your style of dance to make sure it is not considered offensive to others. Your dance must not just edify you, but others as well. Avoid dancing in a manner that considered sexually suggestive in certain context~(such as African dance Kwasakwasa—a cultural sexual dance, Western pop–culture dance styles).

"Let them praise his name in the dance: let them sing praises unto him with the tumbrel and harp"· (Psalms s 149:3).

As Christians, we do not have a problem with singing in general, although some denominations have a problem with contemporary type of music, preferring choral with a church-organ or sometimes-piano accompaniment as opposed to up-tempo music. I consider this argument about the type of music academic, although it is broad and cannot be addressed exhaustively in this book. The other area we can disagree widely is about the likes and dislikes of different types of music as well as which type is spiritual. Even so, the principal thing is that at the end of the day we must ensure that our praise and worship is not just performance-driven. The difference between a mere performance or showbiz and worship or real ministry to the Lord is the fact that in performance, we seek to entertain the people and is merely fleshly. You personally know which one it is you are doing. If all you aim for is just to excite people, making them feel good or for people to know and talk about you, then you are probably in for showbiz.

On the other hand, ministry is geared and directed at edifying people and drawing them into the presence of God. It seeks to minister to the Lord as the center of our worship. Worship and real ministry come from a heart, which seeks to glorify God. It comes from the heart that seeks to make God glad at the end of the day and not just to excite people. Of course we cannot rule out the fact that people may and will certainly get excited and blessed with our ministry.

We praise Him with musical or sound instruments.

Whilst there are still some resistance and controversy regarding the use of musical instruments in certain quarters within the body of Christ, it is interesting to see that the Bible allows their use. Many people of old, especially the children of Israel used instruments to make music and praise God during celebration of various festivals, or after gaining victory in battle etc. You can use all manners of instruments whether traditional or modern electric equipments. Always aim for excellence in the music while maintaining spirituality of the lyrics. "Praise him with the tumbrel and dance: praise him with stringed instruments and organ" ~(Psalms 150:4)

a) We praise and worship God with the Lifting up of our hands-

"Thus, will I bless thee while I live: I will lift up my hands in thy name" ~(Psalms 63:4).

"Lift up your hands in the sanctuary, and bless the LORD"~(Psalms 134:2).

b) We praise the Lord with clapping of hands and shouts of praise.

"To the chief Musician, A Psalms for the sons of Korah. O claps your hands, all ye people; shout unto God with the voice of triumph"~(Psalms 47:1).

c) We worship the Lord with kneeling and bowing down.

"O come, Let us worship and bow down: Let us kneel before the LORD our maker".~(Psalms 95:6).

"All they that be fat upon Earth shall eat and worship: all they that go down to the dust shall bow before him: and none can keep alive his own soul" ~(Psalms 22:29).

d) We worship the Lord by laying prostrate on the floor.

"The four and twenty elders fall down before him that sat on the throne, and worship him that liveth forever and ever, and cast their crowns before the throne", saying, ~(Revelation 4:10)

"And when he had taken the book, the four beasts and four and twenty, elders fell down before the Lamb, having every one of them harps, and golden vials full of odors, which are the prayers of saints"~(Revelation 5:8)

"And all the angels stood round about the throne, and about the elders and the four beasts, and fell before the throne on their faces, and worshipped God, Saying, Amen: Blessing, and glory, and wisdom, and thanksgiving, and honor, and power, and might, be unto our God forever and ever, Amen" ~(Revelation 7:11-12).

Most of all Jesus spoke about the true worshippers who will worship the Father in Spirit and in truth in the book of John 4: 23-24. Here our Lord also mentions that it is not about the direction or place that determines the acceptability of our worship. This then confirms to us that there must be something more than a specific direction or place. Thus, we need to learn what worshipping the Lord in spirit and truth really is.

God is seeking true worshipers. It is our responsibility to discover, learn, and embrace the proper way of worship. I have made a few observations that might help us as we seek to develop intimacy with God and experience His tangible manifest presence for empowerment.

How to keep your focus during worship

When you are blindly walloping around in darkness and ingrained in a spirit of religion you can always make a fuss about anything. I had a problem with those who prayed with their eyes open, until I came to know that there is nothing wrong with keeping eyes open when praying. I have come to realize that every individual has his or her own concentration span. For example, for some people worshipping with their eyes open is perfectly fine, and yet, for others it does not work. As for me, I have discovered, not as a general rule, that when I worship with my eyes closed, I am able to concentrate better; it helps me keep out the natural surroundings and things that would otherwise, easily distract my attention and focus. With my eyes closed during worship, I care less and less about my immediate environment—the people around me are no longer a distraction.

It is true for many people that as worship progresses with eyes closed their ability to concentrate on the Lord is enhanced. This opens your mind and spirit to the Lord that you can actually visualize the Lord in His glory and power. The best is always to try and picture the Lord as seated at the right hand of the God's majesty. This helps to bring your spirit man in tune with the Lord. It creates room allowing the Holy Spirit to take you deeper into the presence of the Lord. That is where we can truly worship the Lord in spirit and in truth—where our mouths speak for our hearts in union with our spirits in worship. That is why there is a great difference between singing from a songbook and praising the Lord from the heart. I know for others it is easy to sing from their hearts while reading from a song book or from a wide projection screen, yet, many find it hard to connect their hearts, minds, and mouth as they do it simultaneously.

<><><>

CHAPTER 4

ALLOW THE LORD THE LIBERTY AND TIME IN WORSHIP

We must understand that each meeting is different. No single meeting is the same as the other, because God has a unique package for each meeting. God has a different blessing, a different word for His children every time they meet. Know that God wants to reveal Himself in a different way. He desires to move among His people in a different way, different from the way He moved yesterday. God desires to visit us in a different way, a new way with a new anointing, a new experience of His presence, a refreshing and a refilling, a new wine, a fresh anointing, God wants to manifest Himself in a new way each time we gather. That is why we need to be sensitive to be careful not to limit or hinder His flow in our midst. We need to allow for liberality during worship.

God will only have the liberty to flow by His Holy Spirit in a worship service in proportional to the liberty and freedom with which we allow Him to operate and minister to us. If we draw nigh to Him, He has promised to draw nigh to us. God will move in the midst of His people based on the devotion and brokenness of our hearts in worship. James 4:8 says, "Draw near to God, and He will draw near to you..."

The more devoted and totally sold-out we are to Him, the more we will experience His presence in an unprecedented way. The more undivided attention and time we give Him, the greater the release of His Holy Spirit during our praise and worship time.

We are living in the time when people are getting too busy with life schedules. This places a strenuous demand on their available time a result. Busyness has necessitated a need for a much faster, quicker way of getting things done without spending too much of their scarce commodity. That is why there is an increased demand for fast food, ready-made food, and instant things like instant-coffee, instant-tea and the list is endless. The food industry is good at meeting these ever increasing needs. They have innovatively tailored their products and services for such busy people such as drive-thru, take-away or to-go, to meet the need for convenience; especially for those who do not have the time to sit and dine in places like the restaurants. People on the-go, those always on the move; they would rather eat as they drive. This has evolved into a culture, which has polluted our minds to the extent that when we come in church all we want to do is rush through the service. We want to rush God through in the worship, sing one or two choruses and one worship song. We even tell God that if He does not show up within a certain time we will be going home. Yet we can spend hours and hours in watching TV, a movie or surfing the web, but we spend five minutes in His presence. The love for God in many people's lives is diminishing and waxing cold as we are approaching the end of times just like Jesus said. We need God's grace in this area so that in the midst of our busy schedule we can still allocate God His own time: a time to commune with our Creator, our Heavenly Father.

> "The more time we spend in worship before God, the more our relationship with the Holy Spirit develops, and the more we will experience the power of His presence"

The Lord God desires that we spend quality time with Him. God desires that we learn to be in His presence where we can be alone with Him. He longs for an intimate relationship with us as His children. Where we can talk to

Him like Moses did in the ancient days where God spoke to Him as a man speaks to his friend.

Be sensitive to the move of the Holy Spirit

The church leadership needs to be sensitive enough not to be too much time conscious or so rigid to the extent that we do not give God the liberty to move as He desires in the congregation. I strongly believe one of the reasons we must meet regularly as a church be it on a Sunday or mid week service is firstly, to be perfected in holiness and equipped for service through the by learning the Word of God. "And He gave some Apostle, pastors, prophets, evangelist, teachers …for the perfecting and equipping of the saints for the work of the ministry…"~(Ephesians 4 : 11-12).

And secondly, and most importantly, it is a special time for us to celebrate God's goodness. It is a time when we thank God for the many great things He has done in our lives individually. We meet corporately as a body of believers to lift up one voice of praise to God. This is a moment when we all collectively, yet, individually express our gratitude to God for the good things He has done for us while we were away from each other. It is a time of a shared, unified praise and worship.

Many times the leaders in church congregations if they are not very sensitive to the Holy Spirit tend to limit the liberty of the spirit during church service. They tend to restrict the move of the Holy Spirit as He desires during the worship service. This is done through their impulse to rush through the service. The leaders will often, curtail the worship in most cases even when they evidently sense that God is about to do something.

Unfortunately, they even stop the worship prematurely even when they strongly feel that the Lord is up to doing something. They do this in a bid to fulfill all the items on the program for the service. They will take their time in observing all the protocols, expound on all announcements for the day even though they are carried in their regular Sunday service brochure. The convenor or director of the service usually makes unnecessary, redundant comments on almost every activity on the programs each time they come up front. They often seem to be drawn by their desire to stand at the pulpit to preach the word of the very same God they deny ample worship time. They do this so that they do not prepare their sermons for the intended day in vain.

It is not surprising that after such preaching you see very little or no power or miracles, signs and wonders accompanying the message. They may preach an eloquent, well, outlined message, with very little impact, little or no results. These messages are usually the good-to-hear, exciting type of messages, which leaves, no lasting change or transforming mark in the lives of the hearers. The hard-truth is that all that the church takes home with them is a good feeling, a little excitement, and an appraisal that says, it was a good sermon. All you get as a preacher is the sweat and maybe a horse voice. If the churches continue in such routines the spirit of religiosity begins to cross its threshold until there is no real manifestation of the presence of God. This is because we want to do it in our own strength. Remember whenever we quench the Holy Spirit; we cannot expect Him to do miracles, signs and wonders at the same time. This could be the reason there is a perpetual diminishing or disappearance of demonstration of the power of God in some of our churches today.

Allow the Holy Spirit the liberty to flow
This could very well be the reason people who have witnessed diverse kinds of miracles in their meetings are those who have learned to allow the Holy Spirit the liberty and time during worship time. The more time we spend in worship before God, the more our relationship with the

Holy Spirit develops and the more we will experience the power of His presence.

Why do we have so many sick, weak Christians in some congregations or churches today? Sadly, we have people come in the church sick and return home the same way they came.

Miracles will only take place where the Holy Spirit is present in His glorious power. He inhabits the praises of His people. Remember where the Spirit of the Lord is there is liberty—The liberty from bondages of the devil such as sickness, diseases, oppressions, poverty and lack. I believe those who will spend more time in the presence of God will experience the power of His presence that will revolutionize their lives.

◇◇◇

CHAPTER 5

THE PRESENCE OF THE LORD COMES WITH THE BLESSING OF THE LORD.

There is one side of the Ark of the Covenant which is talked about most frequently in the church today. Majority of messages center around it—that is blessing and prosperity.

I believe there is a blessing which will come upon people that will spend time in the presence of the Lord in praise and worship; because the presence of God brings with it blessings of the Lord. This is in part what Jesus talked about when he said, seek ye first the Kingdom of God then all these things shall be added unto you. (Matthew 6:33).

In the Old Testament remember that the Ark of the Covenant also represented God's presence. The Ark of God's covenant meant the presence of God was among the Israelites.

The Philistines captured the Ark of Covenant from the Kirjath-Jearim of Judah taking it to Gaza. When they took it to Gaza, they suffered various plagues such as tumors, boils from the Lord. They tried to move it to another city, but in spite of where they took it, the plagues continued until they were forced to send it back to Israel having consulted among their priests and diviners. The full account of this story is found in I Samuel 6: 1-21 but for our study I have picked some of the verses from it:

"..What shall we do with the ark of the Lord? Tell us how we should send it to its place." So they said, "If you send away the ark of the God of Israel, do not send it empty; but by all means return it to Him with a trespass offering. Then you will be healed, and it will be known to you why His hand is not removed from you." "Now

43

therefore, make a new cart, take two milk cows which have never been yoked, and hitch the cows to the cart; and take their calves home, away from them". Then take the ark of the Lord and set it on the cart; and put the articles of gold which you are returning to Him as a trespass offering in a chest by its side. Then send it away, and let it go. Then the men did so; they took two milk cows and hitched them to the cart, and shut up their calves at home. And they set the ark of the Lord on the cart, and the chest with the gold rats and the images of their tumors. Now the people of Beth-Shemesh were reaping their wheat harvest in the valley; and they lifted their eyes and saw the ark, and rejoiced to see it…The Levites took down the ark of the Lord and the chest that was with it, in which the articles of gold were, and put them on the large stone. Then the men of Beth-Shemesh offered burnt offerings and made sacrifices the same day to the Lord….Then He struck the men of Beth Shemesh, , because they had looked into the ark of the Lord. He struck fifty thousand and seventy men of the people, and the people lamented, because the Lord had struck the people with a great slaughter. 20. And the men of Beth Shemesh said, "Who is able to stand before this holy Lord God? And to whom shall it(Ark) go up from us?" So they sent messengers to the inhabitants of Kirjath Jearim, saying, "The Philistines have brought back the ark of the Lord; come down and take it up with you""
    ~(I Samuel 6: 1,3,7-11,13-20).

Then David heard that the Ark of the Covenant was now with the inhabitants of Kirjath Jearim, saying, "The Philistines have brought back the ark of the Lord; come down and take it up with you" He decided to go and get the Ark to the City of David, Jerusalem:

"So they carried the ark of God on a new cart from the house of Abinadab, and Uzza and Ahio drove the cart.

Then David and all Israel played music before God with all their might, with singing, on harps, on stringed instruments, on tambourines, on cymbals, and with trumpets. And when they came to Chidon's threshing floor, Uzza put out his hand to hold the ark, for the oxen stumbled. Then the anger of the Lord was aroused against Uzza, and He struck him , because he put his hand to the ark; and he died there before God"~(I Chronicles 13: 7-14).

David was so angry and terrified, because of the Lord's judgment with which He struck Uzza, when he attempted to help the Ark from falling after the oxen had stumbled. King David became so afraid that he refused to proceed with the Ark of the Covenant with him to Jerusalem.

"And David became angry, because of the Lord's outbreak against Uzza; therefore, that place is called Perez Uzza to this day. David was afraid of God that day, saying, "How can I bring the ark of God to me?" And David would not move the ark with him into the City of David, but took it aside into the house of Obed-Edom the Gittite" ~(I Chronicles 7:11-13).

However, there was a man who knew what the presence of God was. This man was willing to accept and take the unusual Ark to his house, and his name was called Obededom. The Bible records that after a space of only three months his entire house and all that pertain to him was completely prospered and transformed by the Lord. 1 Chronicles 13: 14 says "And the Ark remained with the family of Obededom in his house for three months and the Lord blessed the house of Obededom" And all he had was greatly blessed by the Lord.

The Ark of the Covenant made a difference in the life and family of Obed-edom the Gittite. The presence of the Lord brought an unusual revolution in his life; it affected everything connected to him. And all he had was greatly

45

blessed by the Lord. Suddenly there was fruitfulness, progress and prosperity in his household. It was as if there was an open heaven over his head. Everything he touched prospered; productivity ensued in all his undertakings. If there were some feeble, sick people or livestock in his home, they were revitalized with good health. This means that if he had some projects, business, which were collapsing, they suddenly became a success.

Obededom was so blessed of God to the extent that it came to David's attention, and he then decided to seek counsel on how he was to bring the Ark to the city of David. This was no small blessing, to the magnitude that the news got the attention of King David. Mind you, David as King he was already wealthy. He had riches as you can imagine; having all the gold, the silver, livestock and everything you can think of. But Obededom was so blessed that David could not ignore, but took notice of it. This is interesting, because David as king realized that he could not do without the presence of the Lord and His continued blessing which came with this Ark.

If we want meaningful blessing, we have got to seek the Ark of God, the very presence of the Almighty God to abide with us in our homes, families, businesses, and ministries and in everything that we do. It is only the blessing of the Lord which makes the heart rich and does not add sorrow to it. "The blessing of the Lord it makes ~(truly) rich and He adds no sorrow to it"~(Proverbs 10: 22).

If we seek riches and wealth outside the Lord through wicked, dishonest and crooked means, they can only counterfeit the genuine blessing of the Lord, but for a short season. It will soon vanish like dew on grass vanishes before the noonday. It does not matter how good and attractive it may look. It does not matter what name one has made themselves in society by reason of their wealth. The day will come when all that will be left of him shall be the tale – that says "Mr. so and so was"...all shall be history for the future generations... no real legacy will remain after their death. They will surely leave no inheritance for their children's children. On the contrary, the genuine blessing of the Lord will abound forever and will increase the more, because, whatever the Lord does stands forever. It is said of Isaac; "Then Isaac sowed seed in that same land and received in the same year a hundred times as much as he had planted, and the Lord favored him with blessings...and the man became great and gained more and more until he became very wealthy and distinguished ~(Genesis 26: 12 – 13).

This man, Isaac was so greatly blessed by the Lord in everything. You will see there were no diminishing returns in his life as the Bible records that he progressively grew prosperous. That is the blessing of the Lord; I look forward to a glorious church, the body of believers who will be greatly blessed in these last days before the soon return of our Lord and Savior Jesus Christ. These are the people who will be very enterprising and industrious. They shall be so blessed with much wealth and riches not just for themselves, but for the sake of financing the work of God. These are they which favor His righteous call. We must preach to the whole world, the Muslim world in North Africa, Far East, and the many unreached people in remote parts of the world Africa and Russia.

You may wish to know that out of the World's population of almost 7 Billion; almost a billion people are living in Africa, a little over 4 billion people in Asia and the Far–East alone, and the balance is spread between people living in Americas and other Islands with 85% majority still bound in false religion and darkness. These are people who have not come to a personal faith in Jesus. They have not come to the knowledge of Jesus Christ as Savior and Lord. Many of these people are still unreached with the gospel. They are dying without getting an opportunity to hear the Word of God which brings salvation.

Remember we must do the work of God while it is still day for night comes when no man can work. Your daytime may be now when you have the money and resources with which you can give to the work of the Lord. It may be that you, as an individual cannot personally go, but your money can go where you may never reach yourself. Your money can go far than you can ever imagine and get somebody saved in the remotest parts of Africa or Asia. These are places you may never reach yourself in your lifetime. God will tell you someday when we get to heaven, "well done thou good and faithful servant". You will be shocked to be welcomed into heaven by somebody who got saved as a result of your financial seeds towards the preaching of the gospel to the world. And in the words of one musician, then shall they say to you, 'thank you for giving to the Lord, I am the life that was saved, I am so glad you gave'. It shall be like a shock for those of you who will choose to obey the Holy Spirit to give your resources and money in reaching the unsaved. This may be the call of God for you into missions today.

Thousands of Muslims, Hindus, and Buddhists die every day without knowing and accepting Jesus as Lord and Savior of their lives. Will you do something today my brother, my sister? You may not have much, but we have got to begin with the little which God has placed in our Hands. You never know how far that little seed can do in saving somebody's life from going to hell.

Remember that Jesus is coming again very soon. We have to do something right away; we cannot afford postponing our giving into missions. Somebody needs an opportunity to experience the love of God. Someone needs to hear the message and to know that God loves them deeply. The fields are ripe in the world. Will you say yes to

God? Are you going to become a part of the laborers of the last days?

This is the true purpose of the blessing; we are blessed to be a blessing to the world. The Lord will truly bless you as you seek Him in worship, as you bring the Ark into your life.

◇◇◇

CHAPTER 6

THE PRESENCE OF THE LORD COMES WITH JUDGMENT

The other side of the Ark of the Covenant or the presence of God which is rarely talked or preached about in the body of Christ is about the judgment. No one likes to hear about judgment, and it is a message which is so unpopular in the church today. There is judgment which comes to those who hold the Ark of the Covenant with contempt. People of BethShemesh at first they received the Ark with joy, excitement, celebration and accompanying sacrifices which is the best you can do when you encounter the presence of God (The Ark of God's presence) according to 1 Samuel 6 : 13-15. But a few moments later you will see that these men began to hold the Ark of the Covenant with disrespect. They started getting too familiar with the Ark; they did something which they should not have done. The mistake most people do is to entertain the familiarity spirit by taking His Word lightly, joking and playing in the presence of God. This is where we lose the respect and reverential fear for the Lord.

Unfortunately, fifty thousand and seventy men looked or gazed into the Ark and the Lord God struck them to death, this was a punishment. In Exodus 19: 21, The Lord said to Moses, 'Go down and warn the people, lest they break through to gaze at the LORD, and many of them perish' - gaze which is translated to intently-look. This means that these men had violated the Lord's command. They deliberately broke or disobeyed this command by intently looking into the Ark, which was forbidden by the Lord. ~(Exodus 19:21).

This should serve as a warning for us today to never neglect the word or commandment of the Lord through all manner of disobedience. We cannot see the Lord's presence, or experience the ark of God while walking and simultaneously habitually living in deliberate disobedience. It does not matter whether we are making sacrifices, giving to the Lord like these men of BethShemesh. It does not matter whether we come before the Lord with joyfulness and dancing etc.... If our hearts are not right, we will miss it though the Lord may not be far away from us, from blessing us. The condition of our heart matters a lot before the Lord. God is very much interested in our hearts, our hearts-obedience more than anything. Do not seek to be a men-pleaser. Our normal freshly inclination is seeking to gain men's approval or please people. This can be a dangerous thing to do and may prove very costly in the end. If you are busy trying to please people and in the process not pleasing the Lord you need to stop it. At time one may give in or serve in the church in order to please man. You need to save your energy and resources, until you are ready to do it the right way unto the Lord. Just like Matthew 5:23-24 says about our offerings before the Lord, "in verse 24-leave your gift there before the altar and go your way. First be reconciled to your brother, and then come and offer your gift.'' This is to save or spare us from doing it all just in vain.

Your outward duty, display and performances must be done in sincerity of heart as unto God of whom we shall receive our reward. The Lord does not take more pleasure in sacrifices than in our obeying Him. In the book of I Samuel 15:22-23, Samuel said to Saul, 'Has the Lord as great delight in burnt offerings and sacrifices, as in obeying the voice of the Lord? Behold to obey is better than sacrifice, And to heed than fat of rams, for rebellion is as sin of witchcraft and stubbornness is as iniquity and idolatry...''

You can bribe a minister, but you cannot bribe God

Many people in our days can compromise in their relationship with the Lord and deceive themselves by thinking that they can bribe God by their huge offerings and tithes. Let alone such people think they can bribe and buy-off the men of God. Some may give in order to paralyze our ability and strength to rebuke and correct them once we learn or discover about their sinful habits or lifestyle. As servants of God we need to seek the Lord for discernment to see the kind of spirit behind some gifts as they are presented to us. Watch out! Because some of those gifts are meant to enslave and control you as a leader. The giving is geared towards gaining control of the church; they may be tailored at controlling you as a servant of God in the end. Be careful so that you do not sell your authority as a leader over the flock God has entrusted you with.

We cannot afford to compromise

I strongly believe the reason John the Baptist is referred to as the greater or greatest born among women by our Lord Jesus, in Matthew 11:11, ''Assuredly, I say unto you, among those born of women there has not risen one greater than John the Baptist'' is because of work he did as the forerunner of Jesus, but also because he preached repentance without any compromise.

John was a man who took a tight hold of the call of God upon his life seriously. He had heard from the Lord and was convinced the Kingdom of God was indeed at hand. Therefore, there was no time to waste, everybody needed to get ready for the coming Messiah. I believe we need the church, the servants of God, and every born-again child of God to rise up in this last and dark hour and preach the word just as the Lord gives it to us. Do not dilute the message to the taste and liking of specific individuals.

In these last days men will develop itching ears desiring to hear what only appeals and excites and entertains them.

In 2 Timothy 4: 2- 5: "Paul charged Timothy saying, 'preach the word! Be ready in and out of season. Convince, rebuke, exhort with all longsuffering and teaching' for the time will come when they will not endure sound doctrine, but they will have itching ears, they will heap up for themselves teachers; and they will turn away their ears from the truth, and be turned aside to fables. But you be watchful in all things, endure afflictions, do the work of an evangelist."

Servants of God please you got to watch out for this spirit of compromise in these last days. There is time for exhortation but the church in these last days has dwelt so much and too much on preaching and exhortations on prosperity. While we exhort each other on prosperity, in this scripture Paul tells Timothy also to convince and rebuke –thus, rebuke-speaks of warning, caution as well, as 'taking someone to task'.

I believe the church must do both if we are to prepare ourselves for the second coming of Jesus Christ. If we are to prepare for the rapture of the Church which may not be very far away from now, then it is imperative we preach the Word of God without compromise. The church must do the work of an Evangelist in these last days. The days of religiosity are over; we must live what we preach and what the Bible says. It time to quit playing church games. The world needs to see the walking sermons, living epistles that represents and portrays Jesus Christ in every aspect of our conduct.

John the Baptist, did not look at people's faces, just like Jeremiah was told, "Therefore, prepare yourself and rise, And speak to them all that I command you. Do not be dismayed before their faces, Lest I dismay you before them" ~(Jeremiah 1:17). He did not look at their names, class or their status in society, be it the Pharisees, the hypocrites, the republicans and tax collectors, even King Herod. John confronted and rebuked Herod for his

54

adulterous life, because he had taken his brother's wife to himself as his own wife. And this ended up costing John the Baptist his life ~(Matthew 14: 1-12).

◇◇◇

CHAPTER 7

IT IS TIME TO STEP UP HIGHER

I will spend a great deal of time talking about things which we often do not talk about when it comes to the subject of worship. These are things that hinder the move of God in a nation. Therefore, it is time we talk about some of these social, the hot button issues that affect our nations standing before God. I am talking about sins which place a nation under a curse or a closed heaven. Men of God it is high time we stopped our compromise and stand-up to speak the very truth of God's Word as it is given to us by God. Today many preachers dilute the word of God to people's taste as if it was a juice concentrates. But it is time we give the Word of God as it is.

It is time we faced our leaders, Presidents, senators, and members of parliament, government officials, no matter how high they maybe. It is time we confronted evil in the high places. It is time to call things exactly as they are in black and white without sugar coating the word with some political correctness.

There is no regard for God and fellow human being in our world today. Sin is running rampart everywhere. The world is growing more ungodly even in the most of the so-called God fearing nations, including the nations which were founded on Christian principles and laws such as the United States. It is reported that the United States has become the largest exporter of pornographic films and magazines.

It is the nation which has great influence in the world today, and has negatively become the tool which has destroyed the moral fabric of the nations as a result of such material. In the United States today, there is a highest level of moral decay which in my view has been largely increased by desensitization of hearts by removing God out of public life. Faith in God is under intense attack by those who promote secularism and atheism, who are fighting everything to do with the God of the Bible, Jesus Christ and throwing it out of the public discourse and life in places such as schools. They are seeking judicial orders forbidding of prayers in Jesus name on the college and university campuses, while promoting sex-education which has influenced young people into sexual promiscuity, the hooking-up culture and free-distribution of condoms among the underage teen and our youths. The advocacy for sex-education which focuses on the so-called safe-sex which encourages the use of condoms as opposed to abstinence—unfortunately, this has become a recipe for our young people's increased interest to experiment with sex.

Violence, crime, killing, drug and alcohol abuse and shooting in public schools, hate crime and racial discrimination, economic empowerment discrimination and prejudice still reigns in many communities. I believe the brutal killings taking place on college and university campuses are as a result of troubled minds, greatly influenced by the violent films, video-games, hate books and violent material which have been allowed to be freely accessed by these youths. They can shoot and kill someone without mercy as if they were killing an enemy in a video game, because their conscious has been desensitized. Sin is destroying the moral fiber and reverential fear of God in our society.

Many of our political leaders, civil society and civil rights leaders have been entrapped by the desire for political-correctness and are busy propagating, and accepting as norm child abortion. They have completely lost sanity. They no longer have the respect for the sanctity of life. In defiance of God and His Word, they are advocating for the rights of the homosexuals and lesbians in the name of tolerance, human rights and peaceful co-existence. It is completely unconceivable, to see how our government here in the United States advocates democratic governance around the world, and yet suppresses the fundamental right, the right-to-life to the unborn innocent children by advancing the pro-abortion agenda. The federal government is using tax-payers money to fund some of the pro-abortion organizations such as Planned Parenthood, which is one of the major operators of abortion clinics in the USA, against the common knowledge that majority of Americans do not support use of tax-payers money for this purpose.

They are the very people who are trading down the principle of the right to life for these unborn babies. These babies are not just a mass of tissue or cells as they would like to mislead people. This is nothing other than clear murder, shading of innocent blood! This innocent blood will be required of their hands by God someday as it cries out "why?". They eliminated lives with unlimited potential—who knows what they have become later in life had they been allowed to live. Maybe one of these would have been the one to find the cure for HIV/Aids had they been allowed to live. They will answer before their creator one of these days. Do not be deceived murder is still murder, whether it is done to an adult or an innocent, defenseless child. We need people to speak up for these voiceless children being killed in the womb.

This is not only unjust and immoral, but it is unfair as it leaves the would-be mother with spiritual and emotional pain and anguish, and unworthiness and guilt. Most of these women are forced to carry out abortion by heartless irresponsible men who impregnated them, who refuse to accept and take responsibility for the pregnancy and the unborn child. These men are an axis of this evil, in no way will they escape God's wrath for their hand in the murdering of such unborn innocent baby unless they take responsibility for their actions and ask God for forgiveness.

59

The pro-life, pro-homosexual agenda advocates using government are advancing these ungodly lifestyles in our society even against the fundamental premise of democratic culture where majority rules within the republic limitations. Yet the minority perversions would like to usurp the authority and impose against the will of the majority, against the loud-resounding voices which have many times, said 'a Big No', to legalizing these sinful lifestyles. They want to be treated with kid gloves. They would like to use activist judges to enact through the backdoor laws that support their agenda. They have chosen to destroy the very foundation of marriage which was instituted by God by accepting, enactment of laws and amendments which are in favor of the so-called same-sex marriages, under the disguise of respect for the rights of lesbians and homosexual community. All this is done to the pleasure and at the whims of people who are calling for lifestyle tolerance and in the name of fighting stigma. They have allowed other secret society religions, like Satanism, Rastafarianism, Freemasonry, which are contrary and opposed to the Word of God in the name of civil rights and liberties, and religious tolerance and co-existence.

We need to confront these sins. Why do I say this? Abortion is wrong and it is a sin before God and everyone involved must repent and ask God for forgiveness. Why?, because life begins at conception, therefore, abortion is taking away human life at its very beginning stage. It is a brutal act of obliterating human life while in its infancy, even by advancing the Bill for enactment of Laws or any authorization of embryonic stem cell research. The use of embryonic stem cell is being advanced to destroy human life under the guise of life. You cannot destroy life in order to serve another, against a background of sufficient scientific research findings which have proved that other body cells can be effectively used for the same purpose of conserving life.

There is so much of what I call intellectual stupidity which is eroding morality in our society by irrational reasoning and futility. We must comprehend that God fashions us in our mother's womb once conception has taken place and knits us together. Thus, knitting as a woman or weaver interweaves various threads and fabric material into one big whole unit like a sweater or jersey.

"For you formed my inward parts; you covered me in my mother's womb, my frame was not hidden from you, when I was made in secret, and skillfully wrought in the lowest parts of the Earth'' ~(Psalms 139: 13-14).

What about lesbianism, homosexuality? This is equally wrong and inhuman? This is a very strong perversion and a gross misrepresentation of the creator's design for sexes wherewith he created us man and woman. This is sin before God. The manufacturer holds the original intention for making a product. He is the one who deftly designs, envisage and determines how something should be made; he decides how it should operate in order to meet a specific intended purpose. Likewise, as the intelligent designer, God as the maker or manufacturer, creator of all human beings, both male and female had His own intent for creating us the way he did.

Ignorance of the designer's or manufacturer's original intent subjects the product to abuse, which is simply abnormal use. Human sexuality was created, designed and placed in man by the creator to be utilized to fulfill His purpose through a marriage covenant relationship between man and woman as husband and wife. Does not this affirm the reason God did not create two males or two females. He Himself made them man and woman.

Marriage is designed for companionship between man and woman. It is designed as a means or source of continued productivity and reproduction of human race.

61

This is why God commanded man to be fruitful and to multiply and fill the Earth. "And God blessed them, and God said unto them, be fruitful, and multiply, and replenish the Earth, and subdue it: and have dominion over the fish of the sea, and over the fowl of the air, and over every living thing that moves upon the Earth" ~(Genesis 1:28).

If homosexuality or lesbianism was God's design, how could humanity have been preserved? Soon the world would have come to an extinction and total disappearance, because there would be no reproduction. God placed the ability to reproduce in both male and female in order them to replenish the earth through their legitimate sexual union, establishing their own family unit. Same sex-marriage is a perversion and an abomination before God.

As reiterated in the Bible in Leviticus 18:22 says, "You shall not lie with a man as with a woman; It is an abomination" This resulted from man's rebellion to God. Man exchanged God for a "lie and worship of idols, where with they are given up to their own lust and moral decay and has subsequently become exceedingly apparent in them"~(Romans 1:22-27). But understand this that those who do such things are setting-up themselves for God's judgment. Why?—because no sin shall go unpunished.

But people still have the opportunity to repent, turn away from their wicked ways, and return to God by accepting Jesus Christ as Lord and Savior. It is never too late. We have got to put a stop to these lies from the devil.

I strongly believe that John was also able to confront the people of his day with strong rebuke-by preaching uncompromisingly against their compromise and sinful lifestyles with boldness because he was self-reliant, very independent. He sorely depended upon God for his daily provisions. He ate wild honey, clothed himself with animal's skin, lived in the desert— thus he did not depend on people's hand-outs, or offerings for food or clothes. He did not reside in a rented house where some rich member of the church paid for his rent. He depended upon the Lord who was able to cause the bees to produce the honey. His clothes were made from animal skin from the wild animals in the wilderness where he lived; thus, nobody would have any claim for his support materially or financially other than the God who created all wildlife. So many pastors, preachers can compromise and fail to rebuke or discipline a church member, a ministry partner, who they may very well know is living a sinful life for fear of losing financial and material support for their ministry.

This is the more reason servants of God need to become personally financially independent and look to the Lord for daily provisions and blessings. After all, it is the Lord who called you and not your financial partner or church member. The Lord God who called you is able to supply and meet all your personal and ministry needs according to His riches in glory.

By the way, the ministry or the church is not yours; it is the Lord's church so quit worrying about money to support the church. Remember, it is Him who said 'I will build my church...Matthew 16: 18, "And I also say to you that you are Peter and on this rock, I will build my church..."(Peter which in Greek is Petros derived from the word Petra-which refers to a foundation rock. Thus, Peter was only a portion of that big foundation rock whereupon the church is built. ~(1 Peter 2:5). Peter was to be the first of the building stones, a small piece of a rock, and on this rock (a foundation stone, rock of revelation about Jesus Christ being the Messiah and the Savior of the whole world).Jesus will build His church..."

We see the fulfillment of this word in Acts 2: 14, Peter was the first to preach the gospel on the day of Pentecost. It is expedient for us to know we have only been co-opted into this church building business. He is turning us into the fishers of men, as co-laborers together with Him; He is working through us, and working with us. He did the same with the early disciples and apostles, and He is doing the same with us today. See Mark 16: 20 which says "And they went forth, *(the disciples)* and preached everywhere, the Lord working with them, and confirming the word with signs following. Amen"

Never despise the men of God.

You can easily pick up a curse when you do not treat men of God with the kind of respect they deserve. Do not grieve the servants of God. Even when they are wrong, and have made a mistake, all you can do is to speak to them in humility. It is time we stop despising the men of God, because they carry the presence of God (Ark of God).

Remember David's wife Michal when she despised her husband for celebrating around the Ark of the Covenant, the very presence of God which had brought great blessings to the house of Obededom, conversely brought a curse upon her.

You cannot ridicule the men of God and expect to get away with it. God will always step in and defend His own. That is why He has said do not touch my anointed. Be careful that your words do not touch the men of God negatively in a manner that God is provoked to defend or vindicate His own.

It was not a different Ark of the Covenant but the same one. She became barren from that point onwards. It was the same Ark of the Covenant which blessed Obededom, which prior to that had struck Uzzah when he tried to help it from falling to the ground when the oxen stumbled. It is time we learn to respect the presence of the Lord by living the life worthy of God's calling. It is high time we respect servants of God, not because of their level of education or looks but by reason of the Lord's anointing upon their lives. It is time we live as Christians; quit being all things to all men when it comes to sin in the name of trying to fit in.

<><><>

CHAPTER 8

WHEN DO WE WORSHIP GOD?

Many times we are caught up in the multitude of business and cares of this world. Every day, is filled with what we want to do and accomplish, taking children to school, going to work, shopping, and the list goes on and on. The end result is that our time is so occupied that we do not have time for God.

When things seem not to go the way you want them to or the way you thought they should that is the time to praise and worship God. When things are beyond your control and it is hard for you bear. When you feel like giving up on your dream and you cannot go-on just raise your hands in praise. When you feel like going back, when the battle rages and it is like you are all surrounded by mountains on either side, with the Red Sea in the front, and the Egyptian army behind you, that is when you have to lift up a song of praise to God. The children of Israel, "...were surrounded by mountains and red sea on either side and Egyptians behind" ~(Exodus14:14).

In the midst of your confusion when you do not know which way to turn , when you do not know what to say or what to do. Like the children of Israel, "the Children of Israel lifted up a song of praise in the midst of their troubles, faced with fierce battles"~(I Chronicles 20:22). That is the time to sing and declare that the Lord is good and His mercies endure forever.

When all friends are gone and it seems like you are all alone. That is when you can declare the praises of the Lord on your lips. When it looks like you have reached the end of the road of your life and the future looks so dark. That is the right time to praise God. When you have a sick loved one and the situation seems so hopeless and worsening as each day goes by. When there is no money in your pocket or in your bank and you have no clue where the money to pay your bills is going to come from. In the midst of all your despair, that is the right time to praise Him.

When everything does not seem to make any sense, that is the time to sing the hymn, 'great is thy faithfulness, morning by morning new mercies I see' sing songs like 'The Lord is good and His mercies endures forever back to the Lord in praise.

In the midst of such praise that is when God takes delight to show Himself strong on your behalf. The situations, challenges and circumstances we face everyday will not destroy you, but will draw you to a place where you can have the opportunity to see the greatness of God. That is the time when you will have a personal experience with the Lord, where God proves and shows Himself to you in a new way which revolutionizes your life. It will no longer be a tale of people a far off about the Lord Jehovah –Jireh , because He will surely have been your providence already. You will know Him as Jehovah Rohi – your shepherd when He has met your need, He will show himself as Jehovah – He will Reveal Himself in His mighty power to you in your challenges that you encounter only if you choose to open your mouth and give him praise in everything, when you purpose to defy all odds which call on you to complain and murmur against God.

"In everything give Him thanks"~(I Thessalonians 5: 18).

"I will bless the Lord at all times and His praise shall continually be in my mouth"~(Psalms 34: 1).

Always remember you can choose to close your mouth and shut up your praise, or you can open it and offer a song of praise to the Lord. Praise is not with the Holy Spirit it is in your heart, but it can only come out once you have opened your mouth, it is a deliberate choice.

That is why Jesus said if you do not praise me the rock and stones will offer praise in your place. I will not allow the stones to praise God in my place. I may be bound in chains or fetters or restrained but my praise cannot be put in any bondage.

You can choose to stay quiet and meditate or think hard, worry over your problems or difficulties. You can choose to remain silent, and listen to the pains in your body. You can allow your mind to listen to the voices of your situations like the other prisoners who were with Paul and Silas, they chose to be silent and listen to their afflictions. But Paul and Silas chose to defy all odds against the laws and voices of pains, afflictions and the devil which tells you, "see you are in problems because you are serving your God, see you are in pain because you say you believe in God, see you are broke, because you are a foolish Christian who want to be the holier than thou and cannot lie or cheat to obtain money through deceit and crooked means". The devil will try to make you believe that you are going through the difficulties because you have sinned against God and that He is angry with you. But that is a lie from the father of lies, the devil. Paul and Silas made their voices speak louder of the goodness and the faithfulness of God in praise and worship to the Lord their God. They said to themselves, our hands and feet may be tied, but our praise cannot be chained. They might have put us in prison, but surely they cannot imprison my praise. They used their mouths to lift up songs of praise in the midst of their pain. Dare to praise him in spite of what you may be going through right now.

As long as there is still breath in you, you can open up your mouth and offer God some praise. It may not feel right, circumstances may not appear conducive. Whether you feel His presence or not, praise Him. You may feel like He has forsaken, deserted or left you alone but you can speak like Job, I will still praise him in faith. Understand that God is still in control. He is working it out for you. He

67

is working behind the scenes for you. He will cause all things to work out for your good in the end. .

Worship God in all circumstances

We are living in a time and hour when life is getting tougher and tougher by the day. The fear of extremist and terrorists, the wars in Far East, the threat of nuclear war, global warming of the ozone layer depletion, skyrocketing gasoline prices and prices of almost every essential commodity is going up and seems like things will never get better but worse and will further worsen.

Major economies of the world are failing and struggling, major currencies such as the US Dollar are declining in its buying power.

The currencies of the most countries in Europe are now gravitating towards adoption of a single common currency, the euro under the European Union. All this will be done in a bid to establish a strong regional currency which can compete favorably internationally.

There is instability all over the world. When you look at the countries in the Far East and Africa, many are torn apart due to corruption, poor-governance, civil wars, strife and regional conflicts among different ethnic groups.

The African countries' individual currencies are greatly devalued by the IMF so that they cannot compete favorably against the major world currencies such as the US Dollar, British Pound, and the Euro. Most of these countries are highly indebted to organizations such as the ADB, World Bank.

These and many other problems are likely to pull the African countries closer together under the African Union (AU), and Europe closely under EU even those countries outside these blocks will try to seek membership. All this may be pointing to the proximity of the Antichrist, who shall establish his one world system of government and whose rise will be premised on solving the world's problems.

The diverse world economic and social problems will have a multiplier-effect which will cause a feeling of insecurity, anxiety which will captivate many people. This state of affairs in the world will cause the hearts of many to fail them as well as grow cold; they will not have the strength left in them to praise God. These issues will literally fatigue and wear down people bringing heaviness upon the hearts of many so that they will not be easy to worship. It will be tough for many to continually give thanks to the Lord.

However, what will bring strength and power to face these problems is the power which comes from the presence of the Lord as we worship the King of Kings. The power of the Holy Spirit will bring the anchor of the soul to believers as they purpose to worship God.

All those who will continue to put on the garment of praise for the spirit of heaviness and beauty for ashes which comes when we praise and worship our beautiful Savior and Lord Jesus Christ will wax strong. Praise and worship is what will vitalize and strengthen the feeble and the faint-hearted believers. They that will choose to stand firm in the Lord amidst these circumstances and challenges in the world will get their sustenance and supernatural energy from the Lord. The Lord's presence will continually strengthen those who will abide in His presence as they constantly drink from his Holy Spirit.

The Holy Spirit is beckoning the church, "He that is thirsty let him come". The Lord says to the whole world, "Those who are weary come and be given rest".

Those who will heed His call will receive strength to carry on in the dark times, through the pressures and cares of this world. Jesus wants to bring us to Himself. John 10:10-11 "He said, I am the good Shepherd who lays down

His life for the sheep". He says, I have come that you might have life and have it more abundantly.

Life speaks of vitality, vigor, energy, power, strength, liveliness etc.. Jesus wants us to live life to the fullest and not just merely existing.

My dear friend, before you continue reading this book, if you have not given your life to Jesus. I urge you to consider right away giving Jesus Christ the opportunity to be Lord and Savior of your life. It does not matter what you have and have not done. It does not matter what sins you have committed; no sin is too small or too great that the shed blood of Jesus cannot remove away from your life. "Come now, and let us reason together, saith the LORD: though your sins be as scarlet, they shall be as white as snow; though they be red like crimson, they shall be as wool" ~(Isaiah 1:18).

The only way you can obtain this abundant life is by opening your heart to the Lord. Accepting that you a sinner in need of a savior, knowing that you cannot save yourself.

For all have sinned and come short of the glory of God ~(Romans 3: 23). Only Jesus can save you if you allow Him to. I want you to purpose in your life that you will accept the gift of eternal life. This life is available only in Christ Jesus to all who accept the gift of salvation, by accepting the fact that they are sinners, confesses their sins, desire to change, and turn away from their sins—allowing Jesus to take preeminence in their lives. If this is your heart's desire, say this prayer out loud earnestly and sincerely from your heart to the Lord, read this prayer out loud now say;

Lord Jesus, I thank you for the gift of eternal life you have brought me through your death on the cross and shedding of your blood for the cleansing of all my sins. I acknowledge that I am a sinner, I ask you to forgive of all my sins. I believe you are the Son of God, who died and rose again and that you are Lord. Come into my heart now, be my Lord and Savior from today forth. Write my name in the lamb's book of life; give me the power to be a child of God. Help me to live my life for you all the days of my life. Thank you saving me now. In your precious name I have prayed. Amen.

Thank you for making this prayer. Welcome into the Kingdom of God. God bless you and keep you strong and established in Christ Jesus. Now let us continue with our study. Now you qualify to be a partaker of everything God has for His children. The energizing power and all the goodies that come when we praise and worship our heavenly Father, Jesus Christ our Lord, and the Holy Spirit, who is our companion can be yours. Remember the Lord wants our lives to overflow with His presence, joy, and peace. He wants us to experience His power and goodness so that we may cease from barely getting by.

When we spend time in the presence of the Lord in praise and worship, we avail God the opportunity to reside in the Earth through our lives in His mighty power. We allow God to endow us with His life, power, strength and vigor.

◇◇◇

CHAPTER 9

IT IS TIME TO MOVE ONTO MATURITY

I believe that it is God's desire that all grow and mature in Him. I am sure no parent would take delight in seeing their 8 year old child behaving like a 1 year old.

Likewise, God expects us to grow from one level of glory to another. Our walk with the Lord must be progressive. It is time to grow up, and move onto maturity; get-off the baby feeding bottle and take-off those baby diapers. We need to grow in this area of praise and worship.

Many of God's children know that our heavenly Father seeks for those who will worship him in spirit and in truth. Many believers can quote scriptures such as these:

"I will bless the Lord at all times and His praise shall continually be in my mouth... ~(Psalms 34:1).

"In everything give thanks: for this is the will of God in Christ Jesus concerning you"~(I Thessalonians 5:18).

"Bless the Lord all my soul and forget not all His benefits" ~(Psalms 103: 1-3).

Frequently, we hear the word, but we never put it into practice (Matthew 7:26-27). I am sorry to say that we have become foolish children, foolish builders, like the builder who built his house on the sand and had to face the rains, strong winds and floods which beat against his house it fell with a great crash.

We may look good outside, well polished; we may live in a good house and dress nice suits, speak some beautiful tongues, sing with a perfect voice in church, we may even fall a few times, we may shed some little tears, but after everything there is need for us face reality.

We can shake under the anointing, and even scream and shout the loudest hallelujah in the congregation, but we must not deceive ourselves in all this. One day the rains will come, the strong winds will blow and the turbulent floods will beat against our house (speaks of lives, family, or household) someday. It is not a question of if, but when that movement comes.

Our culture today is such that it is predominantly materialistic. Many have become acquisitive Christians, who are extremely sold-out to a quest for prosperity due to unbalanced prosperity messages which have flooded some of the Television which we have embraced.

Unfortunately, the church has bought into this system—Where some believers focus so much on what they can get from God period. They have a very subjective and unbalanced view about spirituality. Thus spiritual maturity is now based on the level of our success or affluence. The matrix for spirituality is now how much stuff one has. It is sad that it is now being based on privileged circumstances, such the number of cars one has. Maturity must be based on character formed in us by the word of God and not measured by the presence of material stuff because stuff can vanish like vapor.

The rain, wind, and the flood speaks of difficult times and challenges such as marital dysfunction, financial or relationships problems, loss of a loved one, disappointments or loneliness, persecution resentment etc. These things may not happen to us today, or in a single day, but they will surely come at some point in our lives. Thus, it may not be all of these things, but may be that the rain will pour or the winds will blow against our life or it may be the floods will beat against you one day. Only those whose lives are governed by continual practice of the Word of God will stand strong and firm even in the midst of such challenges. When we become doers of God's Word, we are certainly building on a sure and rock-solid foundation. Understand God has no problem with blessing us with stuff or us having material things, but he is concerned when things begin to have us.

Sadly, many people only worship God when he has blessed them with some material stuff. That is where we need to move onto maturity, where we can praise and worship God whether we have stuff or not. As believers, we must grow to a level where material stuff does not determine or dictate our praise.

One area we need to grow as believers is where we learn to worship God whether he blesses us or not. Where we can praise and worship him for who he is. God desires that we learn to worship and praise Him not just because of the blessings; the car we got recently, the new house, the new business or recent job he has blessed us with. Now understand these things are important and are a blessing and that there is nothing wrong with having such things.

But we must mature as God's children, where we love him for who he is to us. I believe in the blessing of the Lord. I believe the Lord takes pleasure in the prosperity of His saints. "Let those who favor my righteous cause, say continually the Lord be magnified, who takes pleasure in the prosperity of His people" ~(Psalms 35:27). God wants us to prosper. Like Paul prayed for prosperity of Gaius as his soul prospered in God ~(3 John 1:2).

I am convinced beyond any shadow of doubt that God will bless you as his child. He will cause you to flourish and have abundance in everything. Just like Apostle Paul also declared to the believers in Philippi;

"And God is able to make all grace abound toward you; that ye, always having all sufficiency in all things, may abound to every good work: ~(2 Corinthians 9:8).

However, we must exercise complete control over what God blesses us with. There is no problem in us getting blessed and having all the wealth, but there is a big problem once those things begin to have us. We should never allow material blessings to control of our lives. We should be able to praise God regardless of whether we have or we do not have those things we would like to have. Having or not having things such as money must not dictate our praise. In whatever state, we have to learn to give God the praise continually.

We need to develop that intimate relationship with Him— a relationship which is deeper than a give me such and such a thing for me to worship type of relationship. This is true maturity and spirituality, building a relationship that is based on love for Him, not praising Him only when he has blessed us with stuff, but worshiping Him at all times.

◇◇◇

CHAPTER 10

WHAT MOTIVATES US TO WORSHIP GOD?

As pointed out in the previous chapter, most of the time as believers we worship God because He has given us some material things. Of course, we have to be grateful to the Lord for everything He does for us. So what is the place of the blessings, the material stuff etc.

Let me share a little bit of my African experience, growing up in Africa, I have learned things which I treasure so much. People in Africa, can go to church whether they have money or not, whether they have food on the table or not. They still worship God even when they have nothing worth pointing at. Some of them may be merely religious, but they have such a zeal for God. I have been with people who come from some of the poorest families with almost nothing, but when it comes to worship they can worship God as if they have just been blessed with a million Dollars.

People in Africa, especially in Malawi, love God so much in spite of the many challenges they suffer from such as poverty. I have seen people with such enthusiasm and great love for God, but yet they may have little to nothing to show— Nothing materially that would motivate someone to worship; if worship of God was premised purely on material possession.

Some of them can walk on foot for long distances just to worship and listen to God's Word. They do not come to church because they have everything, but because they passionately want to see and experience God. I have also met and seen people who are very privileged by God to be born and live in the most developed countries such as the USA, who are very privileged having almost everything—Unfortunately, many are ignorant or they take such privileges for granted. Some who are considered worse off or poor can access social welfare programs, receiving free foodstuffs, free or subsidized accommodation from government. Thinking as a natural man, I thought that these people who are so blessed would be so sold-out to God, of course some are, but on the contrary, I have been surprised to discover that some of them have no regard for God. Sadly, for many of them church is viewed as a waste of time, old-fashion, and a place for the nonsensical fanatics. But I have learned to worship God whether He has blessed me with something materially or not. My worship is not dependent nor is it dictated by stuff God has given me, although those things certainly have their place in worship.

The Love factor in worship

"For God so loved the world that He gave His only begotten son…" ~(John 3: 16).

We are to worship God because we are in love with Him. Worship is a way of communion with God. It is a way of relating to our God. The essence of every meaningful relationship is communication. Relationship is based on communication, if we are in relationship with Him we will be in touch with Him. When we love Him for who He is and not just for what he has done, we will seek to stay connected with Him. We will surely long to remain in constant communion with Him, we will spend time talking with Him. It does not necessarily have to be a shout; it may be in a softest tone, voice, or a smallest whisper. Our God is not dull or deaf to hear. He hears the innermost voice from our hearts, even the humanly inaudible cry of the heart. We can commune with him and make music and melody in our hearts to the Lord.

Worship is supposed to be part of our lives just like the heart beat. I am sure if you are like me you do not take a long pause and plan that 'now I will have a heart-beat'. It is an autonomous thing which happens naturally. Has it ever happened to you that after repetitively hearing a certain commercial or song on the television/radio without you knowing, you suddenly find it playing and flowing out of your mind and it may even come out of your mouth unintentionally? Once we learn to practice living a worshipful life, it will eventually, become natural. So that it will become almost automatic for us to be thankful and take a positive perspective to situations even when we are hit with a challenge. Instead of complaining, we will find our mouths overflowing with praise saying such things as "blessed be your name Lord, because all things including this challenging situation will work together for my good"

Now like I said earlier, I know it is very easy to condition our worship as a response to God's blessings; however, we must grow in our relationship with Him beyond material things as important and needful as they maybe. Our love for God must not be governed merely by the blessings that we have received from Him. These blessings are to help us enhance our relationship with him. In fact, the blessings he bestow on us are to be used as tools to accentuate our love for one another. We are blessed to be a blessing; to use such blessings as tools to express God's love to the world.

Worship Him in the midst of your adversity and pain.

I know it is easy to profess faith when everything is going well for us, but it is rather a big struggle to open your mouth when you are compassed about with the problems on every side. It is very hard to remember so much what God has done for us even in the recent past when we are overwhelmed with cares of this world. We should not worship God just, because of what he has done for us.

This is why David prayed to God saying, when my heart is overwhelmed: lead me to the rock that is higher than I (Psalms 61:2). He encountered so many lows and highs in his life. Here we also see in Psalms 143:4,

79

"Therefore, is my spirit overwhelmed within me; my heart within me is desolate". In the final analysis, worship the Lord because he is worthy.

The Lord is Worthy Factor-*(Worship Him, because He is Worthy)*

God is worthy and deserves our praises and all the worship, because He is our God. We did not vote Him to be God. Unlike most of our so-called democratically elected leaders, for instance, their authority is derivative from electoral ballot. Their authority, legitimacy and power to govern come from the people who elected them to those positions—electorate through an electoral process delegates their authority.

It is not so with God. He has never been voted by anyone for Him to be God. He is God all by Himself. He is self-sufficient, self-existing, Almighty God, the creator of the whole universe. Before all things were, He was. Before we came on the scene, He was already there as God. This is what Jesus meant when He told the Pharisees and Sadducees saying, "before Abraham was, I am". There is no beginning without Him. In Genesis 1: 1 "In the beginning God…" Whether we worship Him or not, He is still God, He will still remain God forever.

"God is worthy and deserves our praises and all the worship, because He is our God. We did not vote Him to be God"

If we do not worship Him, He will never be any less God in anyway. Nothing ever diminishes His position as God. However, we are the ones who lose out on His blessings whenever we fail to avail ourselves or set aside time for worshipping Him.

God wants us to mature to a level where we can handle our desire for prosperity in a balanced and soberly fashion. Surely God desires to bless His children. And He will indeed always bless us as His children. But above all He wants us to develop a behavior pattern of worshipping Him whether we see a materialistic blessing or not. We are supposed to worship Him whether we think He has or He has not given us a new blessing in that particular day. He wants us to worship Him not only, because of what He has given us or done for us, but rather for who He is. We worship God because He is God and we are His creation, the work of His Hands.

Worship God in any state.

Jesus while speaking with the multitudes which had been following him from place to place, who had witnessed him perform miracles. He questioned their motives. Look at this scripture:

"Jesus answered them and said, Verily, verily, I say unto you, Ye seek me, not because ye saw the miracles, but , because ye did eat of the loaves, and were filled" ~(John 6:26).

Here Jesus is saying to them, you follow me not because of the miracles you have witnessed me perform on people, but for one miracle—the multiplication of the fish and the loaves of bread. You will note that many people followed Jesus for various reasons. Some who followed him were merely opportunists. They followed Jesus not for the sake of the Kingdom, but for the sake of food; they followed him for personal and selfish gains. All they were interested in was satisfying their appetite. They were only after what they could get from him.

Unfortunately, majority of Christian today, they are following the Lord just for what they can get from the Lord. Everything they do in the Kingdom is about what they can get in return and sometimes going too far.

Look at this sharp contrast when it comes to the three Hebrew boys; Shadreck, Meshach and Abed-nego in the Old Testament. When the King Nebuchadnezzar had commanded everyone in his kingdom to worship an idol statue he had set-up or risk being thrown into the furnace of fire. Here is Shadreck, Meshach and Abed-nego's response to the King's command,

"If it be so, our God whom we serve is able to deliver us from the burning fiery furnace, and he will deliver us out of thine hand, O king. But if not, be it known unto thee, O king that we will not serve thy gods, nor worship the golden image which thou hast set up"~ (Daniel 3:17-18).

Shadreck, Meshach and Abed-nego's they were determined to defy the king's order because it was against their faith. They were prepared to live out their faith even if it meant death. They determined to obey the Lord than compromise and live. They had such unwavering faith in their God. Life was not worthy living if it meant living in sin. They believed that their God would save them in that fiery furnace.

In effect they were saying, even if our God does not deliver us, we are ready to die than worship the king's image. As Christians, we need to grow and develop such deep commitment to God. We need to have such an attitude even when it comes to giving which says, I know God will bless me when I give, but even if he does not bless me, I will still worship regardless. We follow the Lord, not just for what we can get from him, but because of who He is. We worship Him not because of the fish and the bread or stuff, but because we love Him.

You see, it is natural for me to talk to my wife, because I am in love with her. She may not do something I think she should have done for me, but that does not stop me from communicating with her. Likewise, she does not stop relating to me simply because I did not bring home the new dress she wanted me to buy her.

Thus the essence of my communion with my wife is the relationship we have. It is not based on what I buy for her, although stuff I buy for her certainly has its place in our relationship. It ought to be the same when it comes to our relationship with God. Look at these two scriptures in closing;

"Oh come, Let us worship and bow down; Let us kneel before the Lord our Maker. For He is our God, and we are the people of His pasture, And the sheep of His hand..." ~ (Psalms s 95: 6-7).

"Know that the Lord is God, and it is He who has made us and not we ourselves are His people and sheep of His pasture" ~ (Psalms 100: 3).

I believe our worship must be rooted in the fact that we are in a covenant relationship with God. Our worship must be motivated by our love relationship with God. We are to worship God not because of material stuff, he gives but what He has already given--the sacrificial gift of His son, the salvation he has already given us.

◇◇◇

PART 2 - THE ROLE OF PRAISE AND WORSHIP

◇◇◇

CHAPTER 11

THE ANOINTING IS RELEASED IN HIS PRESENCE

The Anointing for prosperity

God is not poor. He owns the cattle upon a thousand hills. (Psalm 50:10). God has also said that silver and gold is His according to the word in Haggai 2: 8, "The silver is mine, and the gold is mine, says the Lord of hosts"

God is the creator of the whole universe and all the wealth. The platinum, diamonds, silver, gold and oils (natural gas and fuels) in this universe are all His. If anyone finds God, this means that one has found everything there is in this world. If you have God with you, you have everything that pertains to life and godliness.

Naturally, some of the richest countries in the World are those which have some of these precious mineral deposits. But the richest countries are those which has oil ~(gas and fuels) such as members of the OPEC .e.g. Saudi Arabia, Kuwait, Iran, Iraq Venezuela etc.

The Holy Ghost is also represented as oil in the scriptures. So that anyone who has the anointing of God upon their lives will never remain poor in this world. The anointing is not just power but it is wealth. Those with worldwide outreach ministries and are touching nations around the world are doing it because of the anointing of God upon them. The anointing also attracts the blessing the Lord including such as money and wealth God.

The Bibles says "But seek ye first the kingdom of God and His righteousness and all these things shall be added unto you"~ (Matthew 6:33). When we seek the presence of God, we are seeking His Kingdom. They that find this Kingdom find God, for God himself is the King in this

Kingdom, thus, they have found the very source of everything.

In scriptures, oil is not only a symbol of the Holy Spirit but his anointing as well which is also called ointment. Whenever God wanted to consecrate someone for His work and service such as a leader over His people such as Kings, prophets, as well as people that were to be endowed with special abilities e.g. those skilled in crafts, he anointed with oil. In all these cases special oil was used usually made from olive oil and aromas. This oil would be poured out upon these people as a way of setting them apart for such service. This anointing is for divine empowerment for one to function in a particular office.

The Priestly Anointing

Every office requires an anointing which gives a divine enablement for one to function or service effectively in that office. Aaron had to be anointed with an anointing of a priest in order to function in the office of a high priest.

"And thou shalt take of the blood that is upon the altar, and of the anointing oil, and sprinkle it upon Aaron, and upon his garments, and upon his sons, and upon the garments of his sons with him: and he shall be hallowed, and his garments, and his sons, and his sons garments with him"~(Exodus 29:21).

"This is the portion of the anointing of Aaron, and of the anointing of his sons, out of the offerings of the LORD made by fire, in the day when he presented them to minister unto the LORD in the priest's office;"~(Leviticus 7:35)

"And he poured of the anointing oil upon Aaron's head, and anointed him, to sanctify him" ~ (Leviticus 8:12).

Kingly anointing

Kings are charged with a very huge and demanding responsibility. The kings of Old had to be anointed for them to function in that office. Here are a number of examples where God had to set people apart in order for them to serve as King:-

Anointing of Saul as King over Israel:
"Tomorrow about this time I will send thee a man out of the land of Benjamin, and thou shalt anoint him to be captain over my people Israel, that he may save my people out of the hand of the Philistines: for I have looked upon my people, , because their cry is come unto me"
~(1 Samuel 9:16)

"Samuel also said unto Saul, The LORD sent me to anoint thee to be king over his people, over Israel: now Therefore, hearken thou unto the voice of the words of the LORD"
(1 Samuel 15:1).

Anointing of David as King over Israel;
"and he sent, and brought him in. Now he was ruddy, and withal of a beautiful countenance, and goodly to look to. And the LORD said, Arise, anoint him: for this is he" ~ (1 Samuel 16:12).

Anointing of Solomon as King:
"And let Zadok the priest and Nathan the prophet anoint him there king over Israel: and blow ye with the trumpet, and say, God save king Solomon"~(1Kings 1:34).

Anointing of Jehu as King over Israel
"And Jehu the son of Nimshi shalt thou anoint to be king over Israel: and Elisha the son of Shaphat of Abel-meholah shalt thou anoint to be prophet in thy room"~(1Kings 19:16).

The Prophetic Anointing

This is where one is set apart by God to function in the office of prophet; his authority is usually over nations and Kingdoms.

"..... and Elisha the son of Shaphat of Abel-meholah shalt thou anoint to be prophet in thy room"~(1Kings 19:16b).

The office of a prophet is different from exercising or flowing in the gift of prophecy, where every born again believer can occasionally flow as the Spirit wills, but the office of the prophet is far greater than this. Every believer can prophesy as the Spirit moves upon them, but that does not make one a prophet —everyone who prophesies is not a prophet. The office bearer usually flows in an outstanding authority; they flow in the gifts of discernment, miracles and prophecy. People appointed to this office often, have a certain level of boldness and authority.

Therefore, the anointing of God can be represented by oil or ointment, which the very presence of God upon his people. This is also called the manifest presence of God. As such we can conclude that the oil represents the presence of God. It is not surprising that the most of the richest nations in the world are those nations which produce oil. These rich nations have oil (gasoline), which makes them rich and sought after by the rest of the countries which do not produce their own oil, because they do not have such oil deposits.

The Bible talks about the unity of the brethren in the assembly. It is unity which summons the presence of God. Wherever this unity prevails, God releases His anointing in a greater measure. Such as an anointing or ointment which was poured out upon Aaron's head and it is likened also to dew upon the mountains and it says there, where there is such unity, the Lord commands His blessing. This anointing touches and blesses many people.

"A Song of degrees of David. Behold, how good and how pleasant it is for brethren to dwell, together in unity. It is like the precious ointment upon the head that ran down upon the beard even Aaron's beard: that went down to the skirts of his garments; as the dew of Hermon, and as the dew that descended upon the mountains of Zion: for there the LORD commanded the blessing, even life forevermore" ~ (Psalms 133:1-3).

The ointment or oil or anointing is symbolic of God's Holy Spirit, the presence of God and the blessing of God. Any man who will purpose and determine to seek the presence of the Lord will definitely find Him and experience His manifest presence as it will be released into their lives. For such people there will be no lack in their lives because of the Presence of God. You will never know the presence of God if you cannot learn to give to the Lord and to other people. I have heard servants of God such as Pastor Benny Hinn talking about the anointing as he prays for people saying "the more I give it, (meaning the Anointing) the more I receive it". The anointing is not just for you. You can never receive it and just keep it, lest it gets stale like the manna in the wilderness. The anointing is for ministry work; it must be given out, it must reach and touch the needy.

Men and women who will experience such manifestation of the presence of God will touch many lives even without them knowing. These are people who will be greatly sought after the world over. The Bible says in Romans 8: 16 "the world cries in earnest expectation for the manifestation of the sons of God". This is the type of people who have grown from childhood into son ship to a point where God is proud of them.

Wherever they go, they will manifest God's character in all their conduct; they have matured in their relationship with the Lord. They have allowed Christ to be fully formed in their lives (Galatians 4:19). They are carriers of God's presence in their lives on a daily basis. These are they who spend time in God's presence daily, not just waiting for a Sunday morning. These are such as have a continual hungering for the manifest presence of God in the Earth.

These people will be like Obededom who was willing to accommodate the Ark of the Lord's Covenant when everybody else was reluctant to take it into their homes. The presence of God will be made available to those that are prepared to seek after God. It may look like a risky venture to set oneself to seek the Lord and His presence, when everybody else is eating and feasting and you are there in God's presence praising and worshipping the Lord with praying and fasting.

<><><>

CHAPTER 12

THE POWER OF HIS PRESENCE

You will never know the power of God until you have experienced the power of His presence. This is the power of God which is unleashed into our lives by being in His presence. That is where we encounter God's tangible presence and glory through worship. Praise and worship attracts the presence of God to show up on the scene. One way to the power of God I believe is praise and worship.

In 2 Corinthians 3:17 the Bible says, "now the Lord is the Spirit; and where the Spirit of the Lord is, there is liberty"

Spirit of liberty and freedom

Paul and Silas were imprisoned for casting out a demon and preaching against evil gains that accrued to a family which used a girl who was possessed by a spirit of divination, wherewith she would foretell the future at a charge for her master. They were threatened, beaten severely by the city authorities in a bid to stop them from preaching the gospel. At midnight, they began to pray, sing hymns and praises to God while the other prisoners were listening. Suddenly, a violent earthquake shook the prison to its foundations and all the chains fell off of their feet and hands— freedom came to all them.

Paul and Silas had a revelation about praising and worshipping God; they must have known the power of praise and worship. They did not consider the blood which was oozing out of their bodies, neither the stripes, nor the pain and humiliation they had suffered by their persecutors. They were not ashamed to declare their faith through their songs of praise in the prison cell. As believers, we get disturbed and discouraged to worship God when we are passing through difficulties, financial problems, or opposition.

David the Psalmist once said, 'I will bless the Lord at all times'~(Psalms 34:1). He did not say that he would praise the Lord only when times are favorable for him; he did not say that all will be nice and rosy for him. We ought to learn to praise God under any circumstance and at all times whether good or bad. The devil tries to take away praise from our lips by bringing all manner of attacks. The enemy aims to draw our attention to the problems and difficult circumstances, pains and heartache, so that we can forget the goodness of the Lord. The devil knows that the best way to get us continually complaining is to make us concentrate on the problems we may be facing. The more we do that the less we can lift our heads up to the Lord who is the source of solutions to life's challenges.

"I lift up my eyes to the hills from whence cometh my help, my help cometh from the Lord the maker of heaven and Earth" ~(Psalms 121: 1-2).

This is why the Bible says "in everything give thanks"(1 Thessalonians 5:18).We do not give thanks to God for the bad things or circumstances we may be passing through, but rather we thank God for His faithfulness to bring us through. We are thankful to the Lord because we know that all things will work together for our good in the end. This is God's promise to us from His word, it says "all things" (whether good or bad, positive or negative) ~ (Romans 8:28).

You see, the Lord knows the more we major on these problems the less we will remember the past victories He brought us through. The best way to deal with any of the new challenges is to look back and see how far he has brought you, the things he has brought you through. Look back at the victories the Lord has given you in the past. Do not forget how he has brought you through in difficult times when you have lost it all.

No wonder David also said "Bless the Lord, O my soul, and forget not all His benefits"~ (Psalms 103:2). It is very easy to forget the Lord's goodness when you are confronted with today's challenges and problems. Remember this is also the man who when faced with the fierce giant enemy of Israel, Goliath the philistine he remembered and declared the Lord's faithfulness. While the whole hosts of Israel together with their King were running away into hiding in caves and rocks, David courageously stood up against the enemy.

David spoke of the past victories, God's divine protection and deliverance he had witnessed in his life as a shepherd boy. He said, "The God who delivered me from the bear and the lion will deliver you into my hands" He told the Philistine champion, "and you shall be like one of them".

Revelations12:11 say "and they (talking of believers) overcame him (referring to the devil) by the blood of the lamb and the word of their testimony"

Power is released against the enemy when we proclaim and declare the testimony of what God has done for us. This power is released against the enemy when we speak of the Lord's deliverance, His goodness and mercy we have experienced.

When we speak and boast about the great deliverance the Lord has wrought for us, it makes God feel so proud of us. It stirs up our God to show Himself mighty on our behalf.

I have seen as people begin to enjoy some music or song, they get carried away and end up nodding or stomping their feet down, even without giving any thought. The Bible says Heaven is the Lord's throne and the Earth is His footstool, "Thus, saith the LORD, The heaven is my throne, and the Earth is my footstool: where is the house that ye build unto me? and where is the place of my rest?"~(Isaiah 66:1).

I believe this is what must have happened in Heaven when Paul and Silas began to praise God. The Almighty

God began to enjoy the sounds and the rhythm and beat of their hymns and He must have started stamping His foot being on the footstool- the Earth and the earthquake had to take place. The same would happen if we praise God and He begins to enjoy it. When He moves His feet, an earthquake takes place in the spiritual realm. This earthquake will cause all the chains of bondage to break-off of our lives and off of those around us who may be bound by the enemy.

The more we praise and worship our heavenly Father, the more we will experience His liberating power which brings total freedom. You see the warden woke up and wanted to kill himself thinking that Paul and Silas had escaped. But Paul shouted to him and said cheer up, "we are all here". This made the Jailer so afraid and asked, "What must I do to be saved?"~(Acts 16:16-34). This is when the Jailer obtained his salvation and that of his entire household.

When we praise and worship God, miracles will take place. Such miracles will cause people to marvel about the kind of God we serve; this opens a window of opportunity for us to share the gospel of salvation and lead others into the Kingdom. Our loved ones who are not yet saved are amazed when they see that we can still praise God even in the midst of difficulties. This will cause them to ask us, "how do you manage to praise God in the midst of difficulties?". How do you worship God when things do not seem to be working out for you? Naturally, they expect you to be moaning and crying, whining and complaining, but they are awe struck to see you having a smile daily in spite of the challenges. They are astonished at 'how do you can have such joy even though you are going through difficult circumstances? This will in turn give us an opportunity to share our faith and the goodness of the Lord which brings people to a saving knowledge of Jesus Christ. Suddenly, we get the opportunity to see them receive Salvation.

The world does not know the difference between happiness and joy. To them happiness is derived from having material possessions and money in their bank accounts. On the contrary, our joy comes from the peace we have with God. A knowing that our sins are forgiven, that we have passed from death to life.

We have an assurance of a better day, and a better tomorrow. We are not governed by the things or the circumstances we encounter in this world. We have the joy which surpasses the so-called happiness which is based on the stuff which is only short-lived. For most people when their riches and wealth disappear, their happiness goes along with it. On the other hand, the joy we have is based on nothing less than the promises of God, and the faith we have in Him. We can face tomorrow with hope because we know our God is able and is faithful.

We can trust in God who watches over His word to perform, and that none of His word will go without accomplishment. This is what gives the believer peace and joy even in the midst of the raging storms of life. And because Jesus lives, we can face tomorrow, knowing he will come through for us.

<>

CHAPTER 13

WORSHIP LIBERATES US TO SUBMIT TO GOD'S WILL, HOLINESS, AND PURPOSE

Worship has the ability to break the stony, stubborn, and resistant hearts and transforming them into willing and obedient hearts to the Lord. The Bible in a messianic prophecy through the mouth of David, it is thus, prophesied concerning Jesus' people referring to His body—the church;

"Thy people shall be willing in the day of thy power, in the beauties of holiness from the womb of the morning: thou hast the dew of thy youth" ~(Psalms 110:3).

The words "thy people shall be willing in the day of thy power" signifies the effect God's power will have in the believer's life. When God's power is revealed and experienced, all human stubbornness and resistance grows faint and dies away. The hard heartedness is suddenly melted in brokenness before God in total submission to His will. When we come into contact with the presence of God, it changes our very outlook on life. We begin to see things with the eyes of God. Suddenly, we are consumed by God's passion. His business becomes our business. His will becomes our food like Jesus who said, "my food is to do the will of him who sent me". God's mission becomes our mission and passion in life.

The desire to see God's will done in our lives develops and becomes intense. We begin to pursue His will with a new zeal and enthusiasm. Suddenly, we are fired-up to go for all that God wants us to do. Our selfish interests and desires become secondary—in fact; self-interest and self-absorption begins to extinct out of our lives.

Each time there is an advent of the glory of God, His presence reveals to us the attributes of His personality. His character is revealed to us in a new way. His unfailing love, and mercy, justice and righteousness is understood in a new way. We experience that which Moses experienced, after he besought God to show him His glory in Exodus 33:18 and the Lord answered Him in Exodus 34: 5-7;

"And the LORD descended in the cloud, and stood with him there, and proclaimed the name of the LORD. And the LORD passed by before, him, and proclaimed, The LORD, The LORD God, merciful and gracious, longsuffering, and abundant in goodness and truth, Keeping mercy for thousands, forgiving iniquity and transgression and sin, and that will by no means clear the guilty; visiting the iniquity of the fathers upon the children, and upon the children's children, unto the third and to the fourth generation"~(Exodus34 : 5-7).

There have been times while in God's presence the Lord has permeated my heart with His loving and merciful character, which is non-condemning, and in a flash it has literally taken me back in time to all the moments where His love and mercy has literally preserved my life from death even before I came to know Him. The natural response has been a very extraordinary contrite and brokenness of my heart. Immediately, I am so humbled, I begin saying to say to the Lord, "Lord who am I that you are so mindful of me am? Who am I, that you show me such kindness?"

Then in view of His graciousness and mercies, I start yielding myself in total surrender to His will and purposes for my life. I begin saying to God, like Saul on the road to Damascus, "what would you have me do?" (~Acts 9:6). And I speak like Isaiah, "here I am send me" ~(Isaiah 6:8), even without hearing a question "whom shall we send?", I do not wait for God to ask "who will go for us?". But I immediately begin to volunteer to the Lord saying, "Here I am send me—wherever you want me to go, I will go. Whatever you want me to do, I will do".

I believe this is what happens when we are permeated by the presence of God in worship before the Lord. I trust that you will be open to God, in his presence and you will yield your heart to Him; that you will submit to God's call for your life.

Brings you in-line with God's will;-

Doing God's will and fulfilling His purpose for our lives becomes our primary concern. Suddenly, we want to be in the center of His will for our lives. Like Isaiah, you say to God, here I am send me... ~(Isaiah 6:8). Your spirit wells up with a resounding, "yes Lord, yes to your will"

"And Saul sent messengers to take David: and when they saw the company of the prophets prophesying, and Samuel standing as appointed over them, the Spirit of God was upon the messengers of Saul, and they also prophesied" ~(1 Samuel 19:20).

The messengers of King Saul were not sent with good intentions. They were sent by King Saul to get David and bring him as a captive, but they were caught up in the whirl-wind of the prophetic anointing. Saul's messengers began to prophesy, even though they had not prophesied before. They might have been against prophetic utterances, and against Samuel, but the anointing brought them to a point where they did not have to agree with Samuel to flow with him in the prophetic flow. They were instantaneously brought in-line with God's will. They became part of God's will for that hour.

Even concerning Saul, their master, it is written "and he stripped off his clothes also, and prophesied before Samuel in like manner, and lay down naked all that day and all that night. Wherefore, they say, Is Saul also among the prophets?" ~(1 Samuel 19:24).

Here we see Saul fighting the will of God. He was all out to destroy David, in series of attempts he did not

101

succeed in killing him. During this attempt having sent his messengers to capture David for execution, they were all brought into submission to the will of God. God had moved on with a new thing for the nation of Israel. God was establishing a new order of leadership through David having rejected Saul from being King over his people Israel. God had to bring them in-line with His will for that moment.

In many cases when God has moved on and is doing a new thing, those who are indifferent and insensitive will usually oppose, fight and resist it. But as long as it is God's will, no man will fight it and succeed. No matter how many people rise up against the will and purpose of God, they are destined to fail. When God is up to something, no man can stop it. God will always intervene Himself in preserving what He is set to do among His people. God will always bring in-line with His will those who set themselves to fight His divine order and the new thing He is doing.

Worship has the ability to break the stony, resistant stubborn hearts into a humble willing and yielded hearts to the Lord. The presence of God has the power to change us. His presence can soften our hearts to yield to His will for our lives like He did with Saul and his messengers.

Brings a longing for His Holiness

When we experience the power of His presence, we begin to know who we really are in the light of God's glory. When the radiation of His presence penetrates into our whole being; it starts to convict us of our sinful habits, and conduct. God's presence brings us to a point where we begin to revere and tremble at His Word. His presence will bring us to a point where we revere His holy character, and endeavor to live a holy, consecrated life before God.

God's presence reflects His Holiness and beams back into us revealing our sinful condition while drawing us to

Him. We begin to see deep within ourselves as though we were looking into a mirror.

Suddenly, we discover and rediscover who we really are and the very condition of our lives. Our outlook on life changes as a consequence of this contact with the presence of God.

We begin to embrace a greater awareness of the grace and the holiness of God. We come to glimpse with the reality of our own spiritual deficits and a realization of our need for the cleansing fire of God. We share the experience which Isaiah the prophet had in Isaiah 6:1-6. It brings us to a recognition that our works of righteousness are as filthy rags before God. As the Scriptures also says, "But we are all as an unclean thing, and all our righteousness are as filthy rags; and we all do fade as a leaf; and our iniquities, like the wind, have taken us away" ~(Isaiah 64:6).

We cease to glory in our own good works as a means of gaining acceptance before God. The presence of God will always bring us to terms with the reality of our spiritual condition. His glorious presence brings a spiritual awakening, an awareness of our need for God's holiness to be perfected in us. And like, the Prophet Isaiah, you acknowledge your sin and ask God for forgiveness ~(Isaiah 6: 5). We begin to tell God, I am a man of unclean lips and I dwell among people with unclean lips. Our sins become apparent in the light of His holy presence. We entreat God for His mercy and forgiveness. We are no longer pushed to the altar, on the contrary we run to the altar where genuine repentance well-up from deep within us.

A new longing for purity and cleansing of the blood of Jesus Christ becomes paramount. Suddenly, we are now so broken and open before Him. We can no longer hide our sin in His presence.

I have been in places where the presence of God is so real to the extent that people fall down before God in repentance without someone preaching and pleading with them to repent. They ask God for His forgiveness shamelessly as they are no longer bothered by people's opinion. Our relationship with Lord now takes preeminence above everything else. It dawns on us that each one will have to appear before God individually to give an account of their lives. "So then every one of us shall give account of himself to God" ~(Romans 14:12).

We quit trying to play Phariseeism; where we are all about commending and justifying ourselves. Unfortunately, many believers behave like the man in Luke 18:11-12, who filled with pride "(the Pharisee) stood and prayed thus, with himself, 'God, I thank thee that I am not as other men are, extortioners, unjust, adulterers, or even as this publican. I fast twice in the week; I give tithes of all that I posses". When the presence of God impacts our lives we stop showing even in prayer—true humility becomes our character.

We stop trying to out-do others; we stop playing holier-than-thou type of Christianity. We cease to shovel the Word of God to others when it is being preached in church, but we first apply it to our own lives. We take an introspectively hard look at ourselves and not others. We are more careful not to conclude that it is that brother or sister who needs to hear this call for repentance, but we humbly say, "Lord search me, prove me and cleanse me from within" like David did when he was confronted with rebuke from the Lord through the Prophet Nathan. ~(Psalms 53:5-9). And like, the Prophet Isaiah, you acknowledge your sin and ask God for forgiveness ~(Isaiah 6: 5).

◇◇◇

CHAPTER 14

HIS PRESENCE WILL IGNITE A PASSION FOR THE LOST

My friend as the presence of God develops a fresh, deep longing for His will in our lives; it also ignites a new passion for the things of the Kingdom of God. We begin to pursue the things which concern the heart of God. It is like we start to tap into the very heart of God. Now we get consumed with a new passion for the Lord. Pursuance of things, positions, wielding of power and seeking to earn recognition or fame for vain glory ceases to be our core motivation. Our egoistic goals cease to be our drive in life.

We develop a new value system where we purse the significant and not the convenient. We start setting our hearts and minds on things above just like Paul said in Colossians3:2 "set your affection on things above, not on things on the Earth"

We intensely seek and yield to do the will of God at all cost; we yearn for the things which have an eternal value. Our hearts are consumed with the passion for the lost, moved with compassion and a deep desire to see others saved. Salvation of souls becomes our most important goal above everything.

Our ultimate goal is living to please the master and not men of this world. It is high time we stop worrying about people's opinion and cease from our struggle of seeking to please or gain men's approval. What matters more than anything is earning God's approval. We seek to gain our heavenly Father's approval like the one Jesus had, when the Father said, 'this is my son in whom I am well, pleased'

By the way, you must realize that you will always fail to please everybody; because you cannot make everybody happy at the end of the day—otherwise you will develop gray hair and possibly die quickly before your time if you allow men-pleasing to be your goal. When we have pleased God, then everybody will be happy.

I do not advocate hostility; I must also make it perfectly clear here that this does not mean that you must be inconsiderate of others. I am not advancing animosity with people or giving you a reason not to dwell peaceably with others. In fact, God wants us to pursue peace with all men. But our number one goal must be to please God, not the other way round. If we truly love God, we will also love people, and desire to see them saved.

◇◇◇

CHAPTER 15

WORSHIP RELEASES US INTO THE PROPHETIC

People are hungry and seeking to hear counsel and guidance concerning their future and destiny. They always want to know what the future holds for them. They are wasting their valuable time and money seeking counsel from soothsayers, fortune-tellers, mediums, and horoscopes.

> "The reason God doesn't show us everything concerning our future is, because He wants us to learn to live by faith"

They are running everywhere seeking a prophetic word and all manner of things which will bring answers and a sense of direction regarding the future.

There is nothing wrong in being interested about our own future, but there is everything wrong when we seek direction and guidance from nature, created by God other than seeking it from Him directly. Remember God created all things for Himself, to bring pleasure to His heart.

"for it was in Him that all things were created … and all things were created for Him.."~(Colossians 1:16).

Whenever we seek such direction from things which are part of His creation, such as horoscope or our fellowmen such as soothsayers, witchdoctors, palm readers, mediums, and all psychic counselors, undermines God's authority. You need to know that seeking guidance and counsel from such provokes God to anger; "Is there no balm in Gilead?" ~(Jeremiah 8: 22).

The people of Israel had worshipped, sought and inquired from the created things like the sun, moon and stars etc, see verse 2 "and they will scatter before the sun, moon, and all the hosts of heaven which they have loved and which they have served and after which they have walked and which they have inquired and required" These abominable and disgusting acts, pave the way for God's judgment. They arouse the wrath of the God of Israel...

Therefore, God poses this question to His people, in Jeremiah 8: 22 "Is there no balm in Gilead; is there no physician there? Why then is not the health of the daughter of my people recovered? Is there no healing or remedy in Israel?" You see the reason God does not show us everything concerning our future is, because He wants us to learn to live by faith. He wants us to put our faith in Him and depend upon Him about everything which concerns us. We are creatures of faith. He wants us to seek Him and Him alone by faith.

The same question would apply for us today, "is there no God in heaven" for us to seek direction and destiny from His creation? God says, they that will seek Him shall surely find Him, if they seek Him with all their Hearts. Isaiah 29: 13 "then you will seek me and find me"....

Once you find God you have found your purpose in life. Once you find God you have found your destiny. When we have come to know Him, we will know peace. We can then rest in him, knowing that He will perfect that which concerns us, even our very future.

But if we draw our attention away from God in turning to His creation for guidance, it brings insult to God. The God who made you knows what plans and destiny He has for you. "for I know the plans that I have for you, plans of welfare and peace"~(Jeremiah 29: 11).

"No eye has seen, neither has it entered into the heart of men what God has in store for those who love Him, yet God has revealed them by His Spirit..."~(1 Corinthians 2 : 9-10)

It is during those moments in His presence that He begins to move and manifest Himself. He starts to reveal His plans and purpose to us as we worship Him. This is where He speaks to us concerning our destiny. It is in moments like these that the Holy Spirit graciously takes the mind of God and makes it known to us.

The prophetic anointing is released among God's people and some begin to prophesy. We tap into the spiritual realm, getting insight into the supernatural such as seeing visions. It is where clarity of direction is given to the church.

We are living in the most exciting time in the history of the church. This is the dispensation in which God will reveal Himself more to His people by His Spirit. As it was prophesied by the Prophet Joel; "And it shall come to pass afterward, that I will pour out My Spirit on all flesh; your sons and your daughters shall prophesy, your old men shall dream dreams, your young men shall see visions;"~(Joel 2: 28).

During this last day outpouring of the Holy Spirit, direction from God will not be limited to a few people with special qualifications; it will not be for a chosen few. Hearing from God will not be only for those in the five-fold ministry such as Pastors, Apostles, prophets, teachers, or any such people with big titles in the church, but for every believer. It is for every child of God.

God will lead His children by His Spirit. All we need is to be sensitive to His Spirit and hearken unto His voice, even the still small voice and inner prompting of the Holy Spirit.

Release of the Spirit of Prophecy-Coupled with faith in the prophetic

After the death of Ahab King of Israel, his son Jehoram began to reign in his place. It was during this time that Mesha, the King of Moab rebelled against Israel. Then King Jehoram set his face to fight Moab asking help from Jehoshaphat king of Judah. But before they went to battle, they decided to inquire from the Lord by Elisha the prophet of God. They consulted the true man of God Elisha to see if the Lord was going to handover the enemy into their hands. But before Elisha could speak the word of the Lord, he asked Jehoram to bring him a minstrel or musician; one who sings and plays songs of worship and ministers to the Lord. Worship ministry attracts the presence of God, which is God's manifest presence, the Holy Ghost and His Anointing. Here's the story in 2 Kings 3: 13- 19;

"But now bring me a musician." And it happened, when the musician played, that the hand of the Lord came upon him"

And it happened that as this musician or minister in song played before the Servant of God, Elisha that God's anointing fell upon him from above. And the prophetic anointing was stirred in Elisha's life. He began to prophesy (verse 16). This is often, referred to as the 'spirit of prophecy'.

"We are creatures of faith. He wants us to seek Him and Him alone by faith"

Dear friend, understand that no one can truly prophesy accurately unless the hand of the Lord comes upon them, and unless they truly hear from God. No man can be a prophet of God unless the hand of the Lord is indeed upon them, because the office of a prophet or the ministry gift of a prophet carries with it a lot of demands on the office bearer, some can be so severe and at times very risky. Look at verse 15 and 18;

"while the minstrel played the hand and power of the Lord came upon Elisha. : and He said, ' Thus, says the Lord…"

You see this is what happens so often when we begin to worship the Lord in song and playing instruments before his presence. We open for ourselves a door to the prophetic anointing and sensitivity to the prophetic begins to build up. We get caught up in the whirlwind of the prophetic. Praise and worship releases us to flow in the prophetic as well as the supernatural power of God.

I have oftentimes discovered and experienced that the more time people spend in worship before the Lord, the more God's presence or anointing fills the place. His anointing is released and experienced. An awareness of the word of the Lord begins to develop. There is suddenly a perception; an inner prompting of the Holy Spirit, a release of the prophetic mantle begins to come upon many of those present. Such that, people begin to prophesy upon each other the Word of the Lord. Those prophetic words have edified, encouraged and built our brothers and sisters in their walk with the Lord and given them a greater sense of purpose and direction. We need to hear from the Lord on a continuous basis. Our victory and success lies in hearing the direction from above which may come through a prophetic word, just like the time when Judah during the reign of Jehoshaphat was faced with a huge challenge from armies of three nations~(2 Chronicles 20:1-5). It took a word from God through a prophet to bring that victory;

> " Our victory and success lies in hearing the direction from above "

Worship releases us into the prophetic, when we spent quality time in God's presence. The Holy Spirit will have the liberty to flow in the midst of His people and through His people the more we yield ourselves to Him during worship time, the more He will flow through us in ministering to the needs of others. The Holy Spirit will bring a freshness of His presence and power. There will be a tangible manifestation of His presence which will birth a release upon our hearts to begin exercising the spirit of prophecy.

All can prophesy, but not all are called to be prophets, which is a ministry gift or office (Ephesians 4:11). This is why Paul says, I desire that you all speak in tongues but rather that you may prophesy (1 Corinthians 14:5). You have to understand that every child of God can exercise and flow in the prophetic as the Spirit moves upon them. Only those who attune themselves to the mind of the Holy Spirit will pick in the Spirit what the Lord is saying to the whole church, to a brother, a sister in the Lord during such times of worship. It is worship that releases the prophetic flow; it releases us into the prophetic.

◇◇◇

CHAPTER 16

SINGING IN THE SPIRIT IS THE KEY TO THE PROPHETIC FLOW.

Allow the Prophetic to flow

Prophecy is very important to the church. It is for equipping of the saints. It is given to all to help them identify their individual callings. It is given to provide direction and knowledge about the purpose of God for your life.

Have a place for the prophetic in your church. This is where people who have a prophetic call and those that are not called into this ministry gift should be trained and pastored in prophetic. These people can be encouraged, helped to understand how to flow in the prophetic ministry. At the same time, we must be careful, because the devil will also try to plant his own seeds; therefore, the leadership, the pastors and the elders of the church should examine and judge the prophetic word being presented to the flock. Following the Apostle Paul's advise; "so let two or three prophets speak while the rest pay attention and weigh and discern what is said" (I Corinthians 13:29). It is the responsibility of the leadership to protect the flock which God has place under their authority.

One of the characteristic of a true prophecy is that no prophecy is of private interpretation. No prophecy, revelation or spiritual experience should be accepted if it does not line up with the written Word of God. The Word of God, the Bible is the final authority. No prophesy should be held above the Word of God in anyway. Any so-called prophecy, revelations or spiritual experience must have its basis in the Bible. Otherwise, it is to be rejected. The believers in Berea were very noble in that they checked out every word or message brought to them. They were not an everything-goes type of believers. They checked out everything to verify it validity based on the scriptures.

"And the brethren immediately sent away Paul and Silas by night unto Berea: who coming thither went into the synagogue of the Jews. These were more noble than those in Thessalonica, in that they received the word with all readiness of mind, and searched the scriptures daily, whether those things were so"~(Acts 17: 10 - 11).

Prophecy will help us to be protected from what is yet to come. It will uncover the plans of the enemy, disasters and calamities to come so we can avoid them. The prophetic word to the church will prepare and call the church to a closer walk with the Lord. As we get more closer and closer to the second coming of our Savior Jesus Christ, who is coming for His spotless, blameless, glorious bride, the church, there will be more release of the prophetic anointing on many. The prophetic word will prepare the church to take a stand and be a voice of conscious to the world. It is time for the church to rise up and be a voice to reckon with, the voice of God to those in authority and government positions. We can no longer afford telling mere stories, trying to be politically correct, and appeasing those in authority especially politicians.

The Earth is in travail. More extreme difficulties and tribulations, birth pains will intensify, because we are coming towards the end of the age. The world is travailing for the manifestation of the sons of God. There will be more spiritual contractions. But as believers, we have a kingdom that cannot be shaken. Therefore, we must build our lives on the rock of the Word of God including the prophetic. Those who will walk in obedience to God's Word will never be moved (Psalms 125:1-2). You will stand firm once you have embraced the prophetic word from God for your life even in the midst of challenges and difficulties.

A word of caution as it relates to prophecy

"Even so ye, forasmuch as ye are zealous of spiritual gifts, seek that ye may excel to the edifying of the church. Let the prophets speak two or three, and let the other judge. For ye may all prophesy one by one that all may learn, and all maybe comforted" (I Corinthians 14: 12, 29, 31).

Not every prompting we sense upon our hearts is meant to be given out as a prophetic word to the church. Many people have ended up getting carried away, being overwhelmed by the power of God's presence during worship. Some have even prophesied to the congregation what was meant to be their own personal word from the Lord. This is an area where we need growth in the church. This then calls for a lot of patience and learning to take place as we begin to exercise flowing in the spirit of prophecy. If unchecked some of the prophecies may not edify the church, but rather bring about confusion especially if the one prophesying is spiritually immature. Remember God is not the author of confusion. All things must be done in an orderly and decent manner. If a so-called prophecy comes and brings people into bondage to fear or it causes them to depart from the truth it is definitely not from God. Also understand that no true prophecy will condone, conceal or encourage sinful behavior; no prophecy should cover sinful behavior. Any person receiving a prophecy should judge it to make sure it is in-line with God's Word before it is accepted. Apostle Paul once said, "As we said before, so say I now again, if any man preach any other gospel unto you than that ye have received, let him be accursed" (Galatians 1:9). It does not matter who brings forth the word of prophesy. If a prophecy is offline with God's Word, you can with all humility, but yet firmly reject it.(1 Corinthians 14:29).

Often, immature brethren are afraid to confront a backslidden brother or sister with a word of correction or rebuke, they would rather use a prophecy. This ends-up embarrassing and wounding the individual involved if the issue is apparent to other people who know the spiritual condition of such a brother.

If you see, suspect, or have the facts about a brother or a sister's sinful behavior, the best is to ask the Lord for guidance as to how to meekly approach the person involved and help them get back on the right path.

"Brethren, if a man be overtaken in a fault, ye which are spiritual, restore such a one in the spirit of meekness; considering thyself, lest thou also be tempted" (Galatians 6:1).

Prophecy must be given for the edification of the church but not to embarrass the brethren. If we feel the lack of boldness to face someone who has backslidden, the best is to notify the elders of your church who handle such issues.

Singing in the Spirit Key to the prophetic flow.

There is another way to worship beyond the known language. This is what is commonly referred to as Singing in the spirit. It is another way of worship. I have often seen people who strongly flow in the prophetic spend a great deal singing in the spirit.

Paul speaks about ministering to the Lord and singing in the Spirit, when he is speaking to the church in Corinth as he tries to bring order in the church when it comes to the manifestation of the gifts of the Holy Ghost. "For if I pray in an unknown tongue, my spirit prayeth, but my understanding is unfruitful. What is it then? I will pray with the spirit, and I will pray with the understanding also: I will sing with the spirit, and I will sing with the understanding also" (I Corinthians 14:14-15).

By nature we feel good when we are worshipping the Lord with our known language. We feel good whenever we use intelligible words, well composed vocabulary using our acquired language, which may be in your mother tongue be it English, Chichewa, French, Zulu or Spanish etc. The natural mind will always convince and make us believe that this is the best way to worship.

When we worship in our known language our understanding or mind is edified. It appeals to the natural mind, as the mind retains control in the realm of understanding.

I think this is because our natural mind wants to be fruitful, fulfilled or satisfied therefore, there is a constant battle between our spirit and the mind.

On the other when we worship or pray in the spirit, our spirit man gets energized. If we can pass this level and are able to bring the mind down and allow our spirit to commune with the Father as we sing in tongues, in the spirit, suddenly there will be a connection between our spirit to God's Spirit resulting in a flow of spiritual songs as said in Ephesians 5 : 18-19;

"And be not drunk with wine, wherein is excess; but be filled with the Spirit; Speaking to yourselves in Psalms s and hymns and spiritual songs, singing and making melody in your heart to the Lord;"

When it comes to worship, everybody begins from this Earthly realm. Everybody starts in the flesh and then progresses into the spirit. There may be a struggle in the beginning. Many people usually begin by praising God with up-tempo songs, and then they sing some worship songs.

It is usually in the course of worshipping with a worship song, or right after a vigorous praise session that we move from singing to the Lord with a known language and understanding to singing in unknown tongues.

117

Whenever we allow ourselves to go a bit yonder into singing in the Spirit, there is a new flow of the release and liberty in prayer language of the spirit. This is when many experience speaking with diverse tongues. Once we begin to sing to the Lord in the Spirit, in tongues, we enhance our sensitivity by shutting down our natural understanding and opening up to the spiritual realm.

Our natural mind is quieted thereby allowing us to concentrate on the Lord.

This singing in the spirit helps us to pay no attention to our natural inclination during worship where we are always struggling to find the most suitable vocabulary to convincingly express ourselves to God. At this point we allow the Holy Spirit in us to freely flow through us, thereby expressing our innermost feelings, our love and gratitude to the Father beyond what human words can say.

Sing a New Song to the Lord

I know many people are too concerned about how their voice sounds as they sing to the Lord. But there is something greater than just good singing in a beautiful voice. This is called singing a new song to the Lord. This is what Paul refers to as singing, making melody in your heart to the Lord.

It originates and develops from spontaneous, unrehearsed singing in the Spirit. It unearths the melody of our hearts to the Lord as we allow the Holy Spirit to flow through us.

It does not matter how well, or bad your voice may sound to the ears of the people around you at this point. All that counts is the melody from your heart to the Lord. You can allow it to spring forth like a river as you worship the Lord.

You may start out in the flesh, but as you yield yourself more and more to the Lord, it will suddenly be inspired and energized by the Holy Spirit. This kind of singing unto the

Lord requires for one to ignore people around, you it may not sound right, but it will build up progressively. Always remember it is not to impress God, but to express the inner feelings the Holy Spirit only can articulate beyond our intellectual human words~(Romans 8: 26-27).

The Holy Spirit will flow into our spirit with these spiritual songs and hymns. Such songs are usually prophetic and inspirational to the people around us. These songs will bring the sweet spirit, the sweet presence of God. This presence of God will carry with it healing to the sick, troubled minds and hearts. It will bring comfort and encouragement to the faint-hearted.

It will be like a pouring of cold water on a dry thirsty heart. Burdens and heaviness of heart will be lifted away. The spiritually dry hearts will be revived with new strength and zeal for the Lord. Such spiritual songs will inspire people to put their faith and hope in God.

These prophetic songs have carried with them a direct and accurate prophetic word which speaks into the very situations of God's people. Sometimes, it is some of the very old songs we know; but they suddenly carry some kind of momentous, inspiration as we sing them. Such songs carry an unusual freshness, a new meaning, a new significance and blessing.

Many times such songs will be completely new, songs we do not know. And such songs are what I believe the scriptures call a 'new songs' to the Lord. There are many scriptures in the Bible which talks about "a New Song" to the Lord. Of particular interest is the book of Psalms where David talks about singing a 'new song' to the Lord. Here are some of these;

"Sing unto him a new song; play skillfully with a loud noise" ~(Psalms 33:3)

"And he hath put a new song in my mouth, even praise unto our God: many shall see it, and fear, and shall trust in the LORD" ~(Psalms 40:3).

"O sing unto the LORD a new song: sing unto the LORD, all the Earth" ~(Psalms 96:1).

"O sing unto the LORD a new song; for he hath done marvelous things: His right hand, and his holy arm, hath gotten him the victory" ~(Psalms 98:1).

The book of Revelation has a number of scriptures which talks about singing a new song to the Lord as well. Here are some;

"And they sung a new song, saying, Thou art worthy to take the book, and to open the seals thereof: for thou wast slain, and hast redeemed us to God by thy blood out of every kindred, and tongue, and people, and nation;" ~ (Revelation 5:9).

"And they sung as it were a new song before the throne, and before the four beasts, and the elders: and no man could learn that song but the hundred and forty and four thousand, which were redeemed from the Earth" ~ (Revelation 14:3)

Let me emphasize that on many occasions such new songs to the Lord come to us unplanned, spontaneous, and unrehearsed. Of course they may start off from a known worship song-flow.

Whenever we gather for worship as the body of Christ, the Lord Himself enables us to catch in the Spirit what the Holy Spirit intends to do, specifically what He wants to minister to us. It is the Holy Spirit who always brings these new songs to us for the purpose of ministering to His people, to strengthen, encourage and reveal God's plans. David says in Psalms 40:3, "And he hath put a new song in my mouth, even praise unto our God: many shall see it, and fear, and shall trust in the Lord"

I do not know about you, but I have often wondered why our worship seems to be short-lived during church or personal worship time. On the other hand, the angels in heaven never stop day and night; they never cease to worship God. Oh how I long that the Holy Spirit would teach and help us to spend more time in His presence on a daily basis.

A few times we have experienced worship sessions which have gone further into singing in the spirit and singing new songs to the Lord. I have been greatly surprised that such songs have gone on for a long time. Many times a song has been sung for over 15-20 minutes. I remember, on one occasion, a song was sung for almost half hour non-stop.

These songs are usually simple one verse and a short chorus with few words without sophistication such as transpose or a bridge.

Generally, by the end of such worship it feels like you have been worshipping for only 5-10 minutes—time seems to fly by during such worship experiences as people do not even look at their watches.

Wherever this happens I believe it has been as a result of people being hungry for the Lord. It is about believers yielding willingly in an undivided attention to God in worship. During this time people are not in a hurry. The hunger and thirst for God has been unprecedented.

During such worship time people have even remained in the church prostrating on the floor for hours before the Lord; forgetting themselves and only yearning for nothing, but God.

Do you have such a hunger my dear friend? It is important to respect time and observe programs, but way too many times our church programs have restricted, limited, and prevented us from experiencing the presence of God.

Unfortunately, we are too busy with our own every day business, the cares of this world—in the end we have no time for the Lord. It is time to change and set our priorities right. "Seek ye first the Kingdom of God then all these things shall be added unto you" (Matthew 6: 33).

Many people complain about the length of service on a Sunday morning, yet we have the whole week to ourselves to do our business. God is not even demanding the whole Sunday, but merely a fraction of it. It is time we give God His rightful place in our lives, this can be reflected in how much time we give Him in return.

◇◇◇

CHAPTER 17

SPIRIT-TO-SPIRIT CONTACT-CONNECTION

Has it ever occurred to you that when you miss your prayers or reading your Bible, you feel some kind of emptiness in your heart? You may even have a conviction about it. The Holy Spirit within us orchestrates this. God will always communicate to us through our spirit man by His Holy Spirit who dwells in us. The Holy Spirit is always communicating with our spirits all the time to stay in contact with the Father. Our spirits yearn and cry out to commune with our Creator. Remember that God is Spirit and they that worship Him must worship Him in Spirit and in truth.(John 4:24).

> "Our spirits yearn and cry out to commune with our Creator"

Let us examine this scripture John 4:24, as it relates to worship in Spirit. I believe this is only possible when we allow our Spirit-man to rise above our natural mind and flesh. You allow your spirit man to connect directly to Father.

Jesus when talking to His disciples in the garden of Gethsemane just before he was crucified, he said to them, your Spirit is willing but the flesh (meaning body) is weak. Our body is meant to serve and compliment our spirit man.

Although often times our flesh desires and strives against the promptings of our inner man, the spirit-man.

The fresh always desire to sit down and not work, just sleep, doing nothing, but rest, rest, rest, and rest.

It does not want to go to church, and even when it is in a church service it does not want to dance for the Lord, but sit down. It does not want to lift up hands during worship; it is tired always even when it has done literally nothing. It does not want to fast; it is always craving for candies, cakes, beef, and so many other foodstuffs. It wants partying all the time.

We need to get our bodies to line up with the longing of our Spirit-man. We need to be careful not to allow our bodies to overpower our spirit man. You must bring the body into subjection to the desire of the Spirit man within.

We can develop our spirit man to be stronger than our emotions, fleshly desires and will by beginning to obey the smallest of the instructions and promptings of the Spirit as they are placed upon our hearts by the Lord.

Allow your Spirit to reach out and touch the Spirit of God

Our Spirit is always reaching out to God, yearning to touch the very heart of God. This usually happens many times when our Spirit-man begins to travail in prayer, or is contrite before the Lord in repentance or broken in worship. As this takes place one may become incapable of producing well-constructed sentences using well-polished grammar, but end up in tears and groaning before the Lord.

Hannah experienced this depth in her prayer life (I Samuel 1:5-15). When she could not give birth due to bareness, she decided to seek the Lord in prayer while her adversary provoked, mocked and ridiculed her continually. Hannah had become a laughing-stock in her community. Here is the story:

"And as he did so year by year, when she went up to the house of the LORD, so she provoked her; therefore she wept, and did not eat. And she was in bitterness of soul, and prayed unto the LORD, and wept sore. And it came to pass, as she continued praying before the LORD, that Eli marked her mouth. Now Hannah, she spake in her heart; only her lips moved, but her voice was not heard: therefore Eli thought she had been drunken" ~(1 Samuel 1:7,10-13).

In all the provocation and humiliation she suffered under her rival, it grieved her soul, her heart. The "heart" here refers to her spirit man who was greatly vexed and bruised.

The word "heart" in our English translation of the Bible is often derived from the Hebrew word "leb" or "lebab" whenever it appears in the Old Testament and it means the *midst, the innermost or hidden part* of anything.

The word heart is also used very frequently in a psychological sense, as the center or focus of man's inner personal life. The heart is the source, or spring of motives; the seat of passions; the center of the thought processes; the spring of conscience.

In our New Testament the original Greek word for "heart" is the word kardia. It has wide psychological and spiritual connotation. Our Lord emphasized the importance of right state of the heart.

The words Soul, Spirit, heart are often, used interchangeably in the Old Testament. Thus, Soul or Spirit in the New Testament normally means an individual spiritual entity with a material body so that a person is thought of as a Spirit, Soul and body. We are spiritual beings; the spirit part is the special gift from God which gives us the capacity to have a relationship with Him. Thus, man is defined as a Spirit being, having a Soul which is housed in the physical body (flesh) our earthly shelter (dwelling place).

With our physical person –the body, we touch the earthly realm, (natural, physical, material world) which operates on the basis of the five senses.

125

And with our soul-part we can touch the realm of the intellect, emotions and reason. And with our Spirit-part, we touch the Spiritual realm where we can commune with God our Father.

In other words it was Hannah's Spirit man crying out to the Lord for adjudication, to give her a child. Her lips moved but her voice was not audible. She was pouring herself out to the Lord in prayer 'poured out my soul before the Lord'. A child was the desire of her heart. A child was everything that mattered. Her prayer transcended mere articulate speech.

So much of our prayers and worship many times, is merely an exercise of well articulated speech, full of professionally, carefully crafted vocabulary and well-constructed, grammatically correct English language. This may even be done in Old King James version English, such prayers and worship using some of the heavy words, in a seemingly spiritual voice tone such as;

"I worship thee, my Father; thou Art the Creator of the entire Universe, thou Alone Art worthy of Glory, thine is all majesty....etc. It may include some Hebrew or Greek twist to it such worship may look like this; *Thou Art Jehovah Jireh, Thou Art Jehovah Elohim, Thou Art worthy Thou Great Jehovah El-Shaddai ..."*

Unfortunately, such prayers and worship in many cases may only be persuasive, attractive and impressive to the hearers, but because they do not originate from our innermost heart's sincerity. Such prayers are useless. It is unfortunate and surprising how many church forks today have slipped into religious tradition. Many of the prayers and worship in the church have been reduced to nothing more than mere recitals. God desires that our worship be authentic, from our heart.

As a father, I enjoy having a more direct, heart to heart conversation with my eldest son. I especially enjoy his inquisitiveness. When he speaks to me, he speaks his mind, asks questions even though I may not have all the answers.

I love the candid, honesty and openness with which he expresses himself. He does not speak like a programmed robot or with a rehearsed speech, nor does he speak to impress me. He is real and just himself when he speak with me. I believe that is how we as God's children should be when we come before our heavenly Father. He is our Father and we are supposed to be free to pour our hearts to Him. When I consider some of the prayers I have prayed and my worship, it is as if I have been trying to impress God. I do not know about you my friend, but I think I have equally struggled with this persuasion of trying to make an impression to God as well as on friends. We have a tendency to focus on the people around us, other than concentrating on God. When we fall to this urge, creating a disconnect between our hearts and the words which come out of our mouths (Isaiah 29:13).

Although it is a challenge, but I believe it is possible for us to genuinely worship God from our innermost being without any great effort or struggles. We can have an easy flow of worship coming from the depth of our hearts; so that our worship would be as natural, and simple, freely flowing as a true expression of our hearts to God our Father.

When we learn to free ourselves from this urge of trying to impress God, by being real, being ourselves before Him, we will talk to God as children talking to their Father. It will change the way we worship to a level where it will be like one talking to his friend. Soon it will be a heart to heart, spirit to Spirit communion with Him. We will worship Him from our hearts not just throwing out meager words at Him. It won't be just lips moving, but heart connecting with God like Hannah. That is the intimacy our Father longs to share with us.

◇◇◇

CHAPTER 18

WORSHIP MUST BE DONE IN AN ATMOSPHERE OF FAITH

The writer of the book of Hebrews, in Hebrews 11:6; "But without faith it is impossible to please him: for he that cometh to God must believe that he is, and that he is a rewarder of them that diligently seek him"

You cannot effectively worship God without faith. Largely, our worship must be supplemented by faith in God. Additionally, when we purpose to worship God, it is important that we do so not just uttering empty words while our hearts are far away.

"Wherefore the Lord said, Forasmuch as this people draw near me with their mouth, and with their lips do honour me, but have removed their heart far from me, and their fear toward me is taught by the precept of men" ~(Isaiah 29:13).

The Amplified say…. "their fear and reverence for Me are a commandment of men that is learned by repetition ~(without any thought as to the meaning)"

This calls for our hearts and minds to accompany our worship in faith, , because it is with our hearts that we believe and with lips confession is made as a way of confirming, enforcing and proclaiming of what we believe. "for with the heart one believes unto righteousness, and with the mouth confession is made unto salvation" (Romans 10:9-10).

Many times we overlook the fact that faith is an integral part of worship, we always emphasize on the actual act of worship. But worship must take place in an atmosphere of faith, if we are to experience God's miracles and mighty power.

"But without faith it is impossible to please God, for he that comes to God (this includes our coming to God during praise and worship) must believe that He exists and He is the rewarder of them that diligently seek Him" ~(Hebrews 11:6).

Our worship must be done in an atmosphere of faith in God for it to be pleasing to the Lord. Worship must be an act of our faith in Him. For faith without works is death. "Thus, also faith by itself, if it does not have a corresponding action or works to It is dead" (James 2:17).

In 2 Chronicles 20:1-20 when Judah under King Jehoshaphat was surrounded by the three kings Ammon, Moab and Mount Seir (see Verse 1, 22). Jehoshaphat and his team of appointed singers did not get the victory by singing and praising God only, but they also had faith in the Lord and in the prophetic word which came by Jahaziel the son of Zechariah, the servant of the Lord (verse 14). Their worship was rooted in the faith which they had in God according to the prophetic word; remember faith comes by hearing and hearing the Word of God. When they heard the prophetic word from the Lord faith arose in their hearts. And they worshipped God in faith, believing and trusting in His faithfulness, they worshipped God in faith.

Have faith in the prophetic word

You will never experience victory if you do not have faith for it; their worship was preceded by their faith.

"And King Jehoshaphat stood and said; hear me O Judah and you inhabitants of Jerusalem! Believe in the Lord your God and you shall be established; believe and remain steadfast to His prophets and you shall prosper" ~ (2 chronicles 20: 20).

Let me encourage you to open up to the prophetic ministry because I know many who believe in the power of worship, but do not believe that the prophetic ministry or gift is for today. They believe that the prophetic ministry or gifts even the gifts of the Holy Spirit disappeared with the Apostles or the early church. Some think that the prophetic ministry is no longer relevant today. But know this my dear friend that Prophetic ministry is for today as it was for those in the days of old; It is as relevant today as it was then.

It is required and most needed in the church and the World today like never before. My beloved, understand that the prophecy of Prophet Joel in Joel 2: 28 relates to the last days where young men will see vision and prophesy. Prophesy is for the last days, it is for today. If the day of Pentecost marked the beginning of the last days, how much more are we in the last day today after over 2000 years have passed? We need the prophetic anointing to operate in the church of God in these days, because the days we live in are evil. It is this ministry which will strengthen our faith to endure to the end, for they that shall endure to the end the same shall be saved. It is the prophetic ministry which will give clear direction, through the prophecy of scriptures, and expounding of the end-time prophesy.

"You'll never experience the victory if you do not have faith for"

Learn to respect the prophetic mantle

Please note that it was a prophetic word from God that assured these three Kings above of their victory. This is where and when their victory was proclaimed. The prophetic utterance, respected, received and proclaimed in faith, appropriates the prosperity and victory prophesied.

The anointing you respect is the anointing which will influence, shape and bless your life.

"The prophetic utterance, respected, received and proclaimed in faith, appropriates the prosperity and victory prophesied"

I believe this is why many people have been healed and experienced miracles (whether they were believers or not) during Pastor Benny Hinn, Evangelist Reinhard Bonnke, Evangelist Christopher Alam, Pastor Chris Oyakhilome and many others' crusades and meetings. I believe most of these people come to these meetings with expectancy and faith to receive their miracles. In other words they may not necessarily like the preacher, but they certainly respect and acknowledge the anointing which is at work in the lives of these men. Therefore, they receive answers for their prayers, healing miracles and deliverance for their lives and loved ones from God. When people respect the anointing of God working upon a servant of God, they receive their miracles. This is echoed in passages of scriptures when speaking about the ministry of Jesus in reference to his home town, "And he did not many mighty works there, because of their unbelief" (Matthew 13:58). Although Jesus was anointed with power, and had already healed many, but he could not do many mighty things, because they did not respect (or honor) and accept the anointing that was operating upon His life (Matthew 13:57).

Therefore, when people look or consider preachers as being servants of the Almighty God, they undoubtedly receive their miracles. Their faith may be as a result of a testimony from somebody concerning the miracles God performed through the hands of such men. Here's a spiritual principle, believe in the Lord you shall be established, and believe in His prophets you shall prosper (2 Chronicles 20:20).

The anointing you respect is the anointing which will bless and affect your life. That is why it is also vitally important to sow financial seed and bless ministries by faith for therein is your blessing and prosperity. Likewise, when we draw near to God in worship, we must come to Him in full assurance of faith, for it is faith which moves God to reveal himself to His people.

> "The anointing you respect is the anointing which will influence, shape and bless your life"

Worship enhances our sensitivity to His voice

You will remember, in the Old Testament that God's Spirit rested upon a few chosen individuals with a special calling from God such as prophets, Kings, Judges and leaders etc, but in the New Testament the Holy Spirit is a promise for everybody. Every believer can be filled and indwelt with the Holy Spirit. I believe it is God's will and purpose to speak to us directly, personally without having to use an intermediary or middleman. I believe that is why the Holy Spirit dwells in us, so that He can communicate with us in the depth of our hearts/Spirit. In these last days the voice of God shall not be rare because every believer has an equal opportunity to have an intimate relationship with God where everyone can hear His voice.

His sheep hear His voice.

It is time to seek the Lord. We have believed and relied on the ministry of the prophets too much, that many believers have become too lazy, and too dependent upon others to hear from God on their behalf. This has created so many mobile Christians that move from one church to another, one servant of God to another in search of a prophetic word.

Every born again believer must yearn for a deeper personal relationship with God, where we can hear from God for ourselves. Of course God can and will sometimes use other people to speak into our lives. In most cases when He does it is usually a confirmation of what He has already spoken to us. At times it is because we are too busy to listen from Him therefore; He uses other people to communicate to us. When we develop an ability to hear His voice, we will liberate ourselves from people's manipulation and control. You do not have to be subjected to people's control by depending on them to hear from God on your behalf.

What matters most is what God has said, if God said it that settles it. Be willing to follow His direction. You may not have all the details, or information. One major hindrance to hearing from God is that we want to get all the minute details what He is saying to us. God will usually speak to us; give us a word without all the complete or conclusive details. The reason He does that is that we can learn to trust in Him. It is to this end that we can develop an absolute trust and total dependence on Him, so we can continually trust in His perfect love, knowing that He is working it out for you.

We are too nervous when we encounter situation which looks beyond us. We may not understand where God is taking us to, but we can still trust in His perfect will for us. Stepping out in faith at the integrity of God's Word will bring us into His destiny and purpose for our lives. The situation may not be conducive; it might not make any sense. Everything around may not appeal to our natural mind and conventional wisdom, but follow the leading of the Lord to take course. His word may not sound convenient, but when we obey it, it will take us into His destiny for our lives. Do not lean on your own understanding but in all your ways acknowledge him and he shall direct your paths. All you have to do is to trust in the Lord by believing His word (Proverbs 3: 4-6).

We are at a time in history when we need to hear from God more than ever before. We are living at a time when we desperately need to hear the voice of the Lord. We need a word from God in every decision we take in life. He takes keen interest in the affairs of the children of men, to lead and direct them. We should learn to hear from God about our business ventures, investments decisions, even on how to raise our children, even concerning relocation from one place to the next. You need His direction as to what major to pick in your college education. If we can be attentive to His voice He will lead us on the right path so we do not have to make another mistake again.

"We need a definite voice, which says here's the way, walk ye therein, a definite direction from God is an absolute must"

We can no longer afford to waste our scarce time doing trial and error any longer. We need a definite voice which says here's the way, walk ye therein, a definite direction from God is an absolute must. A clear direction from God is what we desperately need; we cannot entertain guess work any longer. We need a divine compass, a divine instruction, a divine GPS- a divine navigation System as we sail through our lives here on Earth. We cannot take another step again based on what God said in the past. We need a now Word, a Word from God for today.

"But he answered and said, It is written, Man shall not live by bread alone, but by every word that proceedeth out of the mouth of God"~(Matthew 4:4).

Many times we quote scriptures like the one above and many others like 'the just shall live by faith' (Romans 1:17). I believe we are living in a time when if we are to

135

make it we will require hearing the Word of the Lord. Get the leading of the Holy Spirit on a daily basis. It will get more challenging to live in the world today and in the years ahead.

Therefore, hearing the voice of God will be an unconditional must. It is reported that on September 11, the day the terrorists attacked the country. A certain man who was scheduled to work at his offices which were located in the twin towers had felt hesitation to travel in his spirit. He did not understand why he had this unusual resistance. He decided to stay home only to hear of the tragedy later on in the day. I believe God was speaking to him by the Holy Spirit not to travel to work that morning. God is calling us to himself so we can hear from him, read the scripture below;

"Incline your ear and come unto me: hear, and your soul shall live; and I will make an everlasting covenant with you, even the sure mercies of David"(Isaiah 55:3).

If the President of the United States of America was to give me a gift or any present, I would love to receive it myself personally than have somebody else receive it on my behalf. In the same way, I would like to hear from God myself rather than have somebody hear from Him on my behalf. This is what Jesus said 'my sheep listens, hears and they follow my voice ..''~(John 10:27). If you are in His fold then you can hear from Him personally.

One encounter with God is what we need; that encounter can accomplish what man cannot accomplish. That single experience of His beautiful presence can accomplish what many years of labor, hard work, and goal getting cannot accomplish.

◇◇◇

Part 3- OUR CALL TO WORSHIP

◇◇◇

CHAPTER 19

GOD IS CALLING US TO A PLACE OF INTIMACY

God is calling us to a place of intimacy where we can fellowship with Him continually. Praise and worship includes the singing of praise songs or dancing, jumping, shouts and jubilation.

I know that we have viewed and considered ourselves as worshippers whenever we have done these things. However, worship is not only limited and confined to these aspects of worship even though, these things are great. There many places in the bible where people exercised these forms of praise, singing, dancing and praising God.

The first sight of the earliest praise in the Bible involved Moses, Aaron, Miriam and the children of Israel as recorded in Exodus 15:1-21. They praised and worshipped God with singing and dancing. They broke into spontaneous praise and worship seeing and experiencing the deliverance of the Lord. They had victory over the armies of Pharaoh who had been pursuing them after their release from the house of bondage in Egypt. The Israelites lifted up their songs of praise and danced before the Lord.

Much of the praise and worship is also revealed throughout the book of Psalms as given through the Levitical priests and David by the Holy Spirit. The other great book is the book of Revelation where we see the pattern of heavenly worship.

It is important that we bear in mind that worship is not only limited and confined dancing, lifting up of hands and singing although these aspects of worship are great. There is another side of worship which I would like us to consider. This aspect of worship is about sacrifice—sacrifice of praise that comes from our lips and most importantly sacrifices of our bodies. (Romans 12:1-12). God wants us to offer to Him sacrifices. One of the best sacrifices God would have us offer to Him is the sacrifice of praise from our lips.

"Therefore, by Him Let us continually offer the sacrifice of praises to God, that is, the fruit of our lips, giving thanks to His name." ~(Hebrews 13: 15 NKJV).

Now let us back up a little. In the Old Testament worship revolved around the offering of animal sacrifices before the altar. But in the New Testament we do not see animal sacrifices anymore. Christ became the ultimate sacrifice in place of all the ceremonial sacrifices and offerings. But I would like to draw your attention further to this particular passage of scripture in Romans 12:1-2 which says, "I beseech you therefore, brethren, by the mercies Of God, that you present your bodies as a living sacrifices, holy and acceptable to God which is your reasonable service" (NKJV). Another translation of the Bible renders this verse as follows:

"I appeal to you Therefore, brethren and beg you in view of all the mercies of God, to make a decisive dedication of your bodies [presenting all your members and faculties] as a living sacrifice, holy (devoted, consecrated) and well, pleasing to God, which is your reasonable (rational, intelligent) service and spiritual worship"(AMPLV).

In the above passage Paul is talking to the believers in the church which was in Rome. These are born-again believers who had accepted Jesus Christ as their Savior and Lord. He is not talking to unbelievers, but to the church. Many times believers live a life of complacency where they think that because they are saved, then they are forever saved and therefore they are immune to failure or sin. We need to understand that it is our spirit man who is saved and

140

regenerated into a new man. "Therefore, if anyone is in Christ, he is a new creation; old things have passed away; behold, all things have become new" (2 Corinthians 5:17).

It is the Spirit-man which is the part of man that was placed in us when God breathed of His own Spirit into the man He had formed from the dust of the ground. This breath from God made man a living being. This is the real person, the real you. This is why man without the Spirit is said to be dead. And it is the Spirit part of man which gives him the ability to relate to God. When we believe on the Lord Jesus and confess him as Lord, it is the Spirit man who gets saved. The Soul is that part of man which comprises of his mind, intellect, will and emotions. This is the seat of character and emotions. Thirdly, the body is the physical outward element which houses our spirit and it is a vehicle for man's interaction with the physical world through the use of the five senses. It is important to understand that the soul and body did not experience salvation when we got saved. That is why the soul must be transformed by the renewing of our minds continually through the intake of God's Word, which is able to save our souls.(Romans 12:2).

"Therefore, lay aside all filthiness and overflow of wickedness, and receive with meekness the implanted word, which is able to save your souls" (James 1:21).

At times we tend to abuse the grace of God. We tend to deceive ourselves by thinking, now that we are saved and living in the dispensation of grace we can appropriate this grace anyhow. Whilst we are privileged to have the grace to receive God's mercy and forgiveness for our sins and whenever we fail God, we should never take God's grace for granted or use it in vain. We are called never to remain in sin wherewith Christ has set us free. The Bible in Romans 12:1-2, Paul is reminding the church that though we are saved we must make a deliberate, decisive dedication of our bodies as a living sacrifice unto God. The word 'living sacrifices' implies that we are very much alive.

As believers we are no different than those who are not believers when it comes to physiology. It is our spirit man who is saved, but our bodies are not. That is why our bodies will must be brought into subjection of the word of God (self-discipline) through self-control as our minds gets renewed by the word of God.

Though we are saved our bodily make-up anatomically and chemically we are like everybody else in the world—Our senses and body-chemistry such as hormones are alive and no different like that of those who are unsaved. I always tell young men and women as I minister on relationships that they must never lose sight of this fact. The day you got born again you did not lose your senses; you did not lose your natural appetites and instincts like cravings or appetites for food, sex, rest and comfort. Have you ever wondered why your body always wants to rest and be on vacation all the time, even immediately after having one? Have you ever wondered why you as a believer filled with the Holy Spirit, you still recognize some handsome men or beautiful women as you walk through the streets even in church cycles? This is why the Lord Jesus once said if your eyes cause you to sin, remove it, it is better to enter heaven with one eye than your whole body to end up in hell.~(Matthew 5:29-30).

Jesus is not prescribing self-mutilation of our physical body parts, but self–discipline and self-denial as the cure for temptation; otherwise, all believers would be disfigured men and women. Jesus brings us to terms with reality that we must not overlook or entertain lust of the flesh, which leads to sin and immoral habits. He demands that we exercise discipline and self-control in all conduct. These members of our body are not bad, but good. God Himself put them in us deliberately on purpose. For example, sex is created and ordained by God, to be used in the right way, at the right time with the right person, but not to be abused through adultery or fornication (pre-marital sexual-encounter between unmarried people) which is very common in the Western World today. It is very unfortunate that in the countries such as UK and America sexual-promiscuousness has extended to what is called co-habiting which is equally sin before God, whether it is practiced by a non-Christian or the so-called professing Christians. And the folly of the hook-up culture practiced on College and University campuses is regrettably and shamefully immoral. You cannot be a sex object for all the boys or men in a bid to get the right one through sexual hook-up connection. The hook-up culture tends to degrade the young ladies and open them up to loss of self-esteem contrary to the claims of the advocates of this indecent lifestyle. Parents, guardians, and all citizens who are responsible for these young adults must take a stand against this culture. The Church must rise up and speak up into this generation. Young folks can develop a right perspective to self-worth through God's Word. You are created in the very image of the Almighty God; you are fearfully and wonderfully made. This means that God took time and special care in making you. You are not a sexual ball for every young man or woman who has no decency to handle their raging hormones or their sexual urges. You need to know that you are specially meant for one special person at the appropriate time, in the right manner. God has a suitable mate just for you. It will take you to exercise patience to wait until marriage.

That is why Paul in Romans 6:11 says, "Likewise, you also, reckon yourselves to be dead indeed to sin, but alive to God in Christ Jesus our Lord" The Bible says we must 'reckon' our bodies dead to sin but alive unto God's righteousness. Reckon simply means to suppose, consider, because we are called to worship God with our bodies as well. And God will accept the sacrifice from a people who are totally sold-out to Him. You must purpose to live your life for God and Him alone. The Amplified calls this sacrifice our spiritual worship; you can never claim to worship God if your personal life is not totally surrendered to the Lord. If you conform to the patterns and standard of this world, you have blown it away. You have missed it. Many times we think that worship is all about lifting of hands, singing songs of praise and such things, of course all these things are great, but more than anything God is most interested in the condition of our spiritual lives as the first part of our worship to Him.

The way we conduct our lives speaks volumes about our character–our lives speak louder than words. Our lives must minister to the world, to the unsaved. People can agree and testify if we are truly worshipping God by just looking at our conduct.

There is a need for you to grow up and master your soul and body, that they can be subjected to the control of your spirit– submitting to the authority of God's Word. That is why Paul in 1 Corinthians 9: 27 said, ''but I discipline my body and bring it into subjection, lest, when I have preached to others, I myself should become disqualified.'' This is the great Apostle Paul, the most anointed of God – he is probably the highly used of God among all the Apostles. He is the one whom God used to write almost three-quarters of the Bible. Yet, he was still human in every respect to the extent that he also faced the same temptations that we face today. Paul had to discipline his own body and bring it into subjection to the Word of God. The King James Version rendering says ''I keep it under'', thus the flesh with its desires will try always to keep itself above, in-charge, in-control of your life in rebellion to God. Please take note that Paul said, "I discipline", "I keep it" This "I" emphasizes the personal responsibility. Paul had to make sure his spirit was in charge, was above and not under. It is your responsibility not your pastors, not your brothers, or sisters, not your husband's or your wife's, and not even Jesus' or the Holy Spirit is. It is your full responsibility to take a personal initiative; you purposefully determine to have your ungodly lusts aligned to the will of the Spirit. You learn to develop your spirit so that it can be strong and powerful to overrule the desires of your flesh. We tend to blame it on everybody else for our mistakes. You are not the first one who is trying to do that- it is inherent in us. But we must learn to be accountable for our actions. Adam was the first to practice this blame-shifting business after he had sinned against God when he ate of the forbidden fruit in the garden.

Watch out for this blame shifting spirit. Eve too could not accept the blame, but passed it onto the devil. It takes a man enough to say sorry to his wife when he's wrong or at fault. It takes genuine humility for a parent to say I am sorry to his or her child. It takes a respectful child to apologize to parents they are wrong or have made a mistake. So quit making excuses for your sinful behavior, take responsibility and make things right with God.

Interestingly it is our responsibility; otherwise, we would have had an excuse. We would blame it all on Jesus or the Holy Spirit for our sins each time we stumble or fell into sin. God has entrusted us with the free will. We are free agents who must master our own 'will'; God is not a dictator. He wants us to willingly submit our lives including our bodies as living sacrifices to Him. However, He does lovingly encourage us to obey Him. "I call heaven and Earth as witness today against you, that I have set before you life and death, blessings and cursing; Therefore, choose life, that you and your descendants may live" (Deuteronomy 30: 19).

You will see He is such a good God. He continues to guide us so we can make the right choices in life. He guides us to that which is best for us. He is more knowledgeable

145

> " A life totally sold-out to God, is by itself a kind of worship which is far greater than the praise from our lips "

and best placed to make the most excellent choices than you with your little brain.

When we have offered our lives as living sacrifice, it is only then, that we have started worshipping Him—It becomes an act of "spiritual worship". This level of worship is far greater than just the lifting up of hands, or bowing down physically because it is possible to be on your knees physically, but yet be standing in your heart. The church today is full of actors and performers who know how to put up a good show. They always want to prove and impress the pastor. They want to show to everybody that they are the most committed, yet they are not committed and wholly submitted to God. "Kneeling down physically while standing in your heart" talks of people that are good at trying to impress the pastor and everybody else but they are not humble enough before God; they are still in charge of their own lives. They can do whatever they will no matter how sinful without a slightest trace of conviction. Their guilty conscience has been deactivated, through habitual willful sin. They are their own masters. They can choose to do whatever they will, whenever and However, they want it. They are simply in charge of their lives.

It is easy to be inauthentic in worship, like a noisy empty bucket, if we worship with mere lips while our hearts are far away. This happens when we worship God while our hearts are not completely submitted to God and the authority of His Word. A life totally sold-out to God is by itself a kind of worship which is far greater than the praise from our lips. When we give sacrifices of ourselves through righteous living according to God's standard. Lifestyle and conduct which is based on what the Bible says. This is living a life which is acceptable and pleasing to God(Romans 12:1), which the bible calls our reasonable service of worship to God.

When we submit our bodies as a living sacrifice what we are truly saying is 'God you are the Master, Jesus you are the Lord of my life, God you alone is worthy in my life, you are the King of my life". Our conduct is a clear declaration that we do not live for ourselves but for Him.

◇◇◇

CHAPTER 20

GOD SEEKS THOSE THAT WILL WORSHIP HIM IN SPIRIT AND IN TRUTH.

In this chapter, I would like to briefly discuss the last portion of this scripture John 4:24 where it talks about 'the worship in truth' since we have already covered the worship in Spirit in Chapter 17.

So often, we have quoted the scripture in John 4: 24, "God is Spirit and those that worship Him must worship Him in Spirit and truth" but I feel not many have taken time to dissect it thoroughly to understand its full meaning.

The word *truth* in this scripture, in the original translation is derived from the Greek word *aletheia*, which denotes, truthfulness as well as integrity or uprightness or authenticity. Thus a life of integrity constitutes our genuine worship before the Lord. This is not so much about the number of songs, choruses we sing and or how much we dance before the Lord. God seeks the relational integrity and sincerity to be in us. Our lives must be transparent before the Lord just like David said Psalms 139:1, 'O Lord you have searched me and known me.''

You will notice that the more committed and surrendered we are to the Lord in our lives, the easier it will be for the Holy Spirit to have the liberty to flow through us and even take us higher in our worship life.

Our bodies are bought with a price so that God can be glorified thereby. I will talk about this in a bit more detail shortly. We are to live a holy life in the community just as we want to portray when we are in church or among the brethren. You must be a Christian in church on Sunday and everywhere you go throughout the week. The conduct of our lives ought to be pleasing to the Lord daily irrespective of where we are and whether a fellow believer sees us or not—Such that that our very behavior itself becomes worship before the Lord. Our life's conduct ascends before God as an act of "spiritual worship" as discussed in the previous chapter. God is not interested in the show many believers put-up on Sunday morning–He is interested with our Hearts; this is the heart of worship. One song writer, Matthew Redman of England a worship leader, wrote this song: "Heart of worship"

When the music fades, all is stripped away and I simply come.
Longing just to bring all that is worth that will bless your heart.
I will bring you more than a song, because a song in itself is not what you have required;
You search much deeper within than the way things appear,
You're looking into my heart, I am coming back to the Heart of worship, for its all about you Jesus. ~(an except)

God is not just looking for outward expressions of worship, but He is more interested in our hearts. He looks much deeper beneath the surface. He looks at the Heart. David once said,

"For thou desirest not sacrifice; else would I give it:thou delightest not in burnt offering. The sacrifices of God are a broken spirit: a broken and a contrite heart, O God, thou wilt not despise"~(Psalms 51:16-17)

The greatest sacrifice you can present to God as a way of worship and reverence to Him is your life. My friend, will you get more dedicated to God? Are you going to live a life totally sold-out to God now? It is time to quit the living a double standard life and half-hearted commitment to God. Please understand this that with God there is no half-half or 50-50 surrenders. God wants total surrender of your life to Him. He wants you whole, He wants all of you.

Elijah spoke to the children of Israel at Mt Carmel during the conquest against Baal.

"And Elijah came unto all the people, and said, how long halt ye between two opinions? If the LORD be God, follow, him: but if Baal, then follow Him. And the people answered him not a word"~(1Kings 18:21).

Quit living one leg in the Kingdom of God and at the same time one leg in the camp of the enemy. Choose ye whom you will serve today, quit hopping between two Kingdoms! You always are going back and forth. One day, you are a Christian, and the next you are not. The true you is not the one we see in church on Sunday morning, but the one you are Monday through Saturday night – the big portion of your life when you are alone and no one from your church is present with you. Playing church on a Sunday morning every week will take us nowhere. For a month you are serious in your walk with God, and the next you are not. God want your whole heart, He cannot shall the temple with the devil. That temple is you; you are the temple of the Holy Ghost.

Therefore, God is calling us to a place where we can worship Him in Spirit and in truth. This is where our lives are authentic and truthful before Him even before we sing songs of praise or dance. Our outward expression of worship must be the expression of our love and worship to Him—Surrendered lives are worship to God.

◇◇◇

CHAPTER 21

WHERE ARE THE PRAYING MEN AND WOMEN?

Bring God's Presence into your home-

We are living in a time and day when we need, men and women who can bring the ark of covenant into their homes. Where are the praying men and women these days? They used to fast and pray. These are men and women who used to spend nights in prayer watch before the Lord. Where are the real men who could stand in the position of seeking God for their families and the nations before the Lord in prayer and worship? As believers we are losing our families and relatives to the enemy because we have neglected to take our position of bringing the presence of God into our homes. Some families are breaking up under the attack of the spirit of divorce. The children of believers are getting involved in drug, substance and alcohol abuse.

We should not blame it so much on our youth; they have been deprived of leadership right from the homes. Boys normally look for a figure-head, role model and mentors in these broken homes. And if they cannot find one right from their home, they follow the older boys and men on the streets. The same is true of girls where women have lost their position to teach and train them to grow up with godly character. The youth need mentors who will lead by example– whose lives are an open secret, open letters to be read by all. Dear friend, actions are powerful more than words. The young generation won't learn from our words only, but from our actions as well. Do not think they do not see your actions. They are too smart to be fooled. If you are faking it they will tell, and when you are real they know it too. When we live a double standard life, they get confused and end up struggling with identity crisis. Are you the kind of man or woman who is leading the younger generation in the right direction? Are you setting a good example of moral living? Are you setting the right standard for morality in your home? What legacy are you going to leave behind when you die?

I will say it again, today, the youth so desperately need mentors. They need men and women of integrity and godly character, who command respect in the society beginning with their own households. You can choose and purpose to leave a positive character-mark which will shape the future of the young forks. The world today needs men and women who will dare to fast and pray, worship God until He rains His presence and power upon their families and nations. We need men and women like Obededom who are not afraid, but are bold and ready to take the challenge. They do not shy away from responsibility, but they rise up to the occasion. These are men and women who are prepared to take a risk and bring the ark of God's presence into their homes. It will require us to make sacrifices such as fasting and prayer, including night of prayers. That is the only way our families, and nations will be delivered from the corruption, and the bondage of sin which has gripped our people. This may not be easy, but we must be willing to take our position in prayer, praise and worship. Jesus said "And I, if I be lifted up from the Earth, will draw all men unto me" ~(John 12: 32).

I believe with all my heart that when the children of God worship Him whole heartedly without reservation, there will be a release of the anointing of the Holy Spirit which will touch the hearts of men and women bringing conviction upon them, drawing them into God's kingdom. There will be a strong irresistible conviction of sin which will draw people to the altar of God in repentance both believers and non-believers alike. There will be a fire which will soon sweep through the churches igniting unprecedented fear and the passion for the Lord once again. When we lift up the name of the Lord with sincerity and simplicity of heart in true worship, His power will be very tangible. As we walk in the streets men will come under deep conviction, and begin to repent even without us preaching the word of salvation to them. Let me blow the trumpet in Zion(church) that it is time for the church to get back to the altar of prayer and worship on her knees. Are you willing to avail yourself to God in worship? Are you ready to carry and keep the ark of God's presence? There has never been a time in history with such a great need for God and His manifest presence like the days we are living in. If we take our position in His presence, He will save the multitudes of the people who are still walking in darkness. Multitudes and multitudes are in the valley of decision they do not know which way to turn. But we are here as believers to show them the way, and not just any other way, but the right way. Souls are very special before God. Are you willing to place the same value God places upon the unsaved?

There is nothing more priceless and very precious in the entire world than the souls. Jesus Christ our Lord already paid the highest price of all –His own life for all humanity so we could be saved. We are all bought with a price, the blood of Jesus. He sacrificed everything, enduring the shame, suffering, rejection, pain and even the death on the cross in order to bring to us redemption by the shedding of His blood.

One way we can lift up Jesus is when we take our position in bringing the Ark of the Covenant, the ark of His presence in worship.

Seeking and Hungering for God

We are in a time when the love of many is waxing cold due to the increase of iniquity and evil in the world today. Many believers have lost the zeal and the enthusiasm for the Lord which they had when they first got saved.

"I know your works, your labor, your patience, and that you cannot bear those who are evil. And you have tested

155

those who say they are apostles and are not, and have found them liars; nevertheless I have this against you, that you have left your first love. Remember therefore, from where you have fallen; repent and do the first works, or else I will come to you quickly and remove your lamp stand from its place unless you repent" ~(Revelation 2:2-5).

Now let us look at verse 2 of Revelation 2, where God is saying to the Church of Ephesus, "I know your works, your labor, your patience, and that you cannot bear those who are evil. And you have tested those who say they are apostles and are not and have found them liars;" God is commending the church for the good things, the areas the church had done well. Please note that God is not unjust to forget the good works we do. God takes notice of all the good works we do for His Kingdom.

However, He also draws us to the fact that we must come to terms with reality. He desires and enjoys our fellowship more than mere service or duty for the kingdom. Why does He do this? God wants sons and daughters who can serve in His Kingdom, but not just mere servants. You are His child first and His servant second. We serve Him, because of the relationship we have with Him first as children.

Allow me to share this with you; when I began my relationship with Budile, my wife, I became so passionate about her. I wanted us to be together almost everywhere. I wanted to spend more time with her. I wanted us to eat together every day. A day could not pass by without talking to her. I believe most of you who are married or have been in a love relationship can relate to my experience. There were times we never wanted to part company at all. Each day was filled with fond memories of the stories and moments of the previous day. This is how passionate we must be about God—Where you cannot allow a day to go by without spending quality time with Him.

Traditions, rituals, legalism, service, and display of performance within the church have replaced so much of the passionate love for the Lord. The service to the Lord these days is not representative of our love for the Lord, but it has become rather obligatory—a matter of fulfilling a duty. Many believers are caught up trying to please men, it can be our pastors, reverends and fellow Christians...they may hide behind service in the ministry. That is where we also need discernment as leaders especially pastors (you may not suspect this, but check out some zealousness). Many pretend to be serious with the Lord when they are with a fellow church member just to please them. We are not here to please mere mortal men, but God to whom we are answerable. He wants us to our service of Him to derive from our love for Him.

I got saved while in high school and I recall strongly sensing the call of the Lord upon my life. I had a strong desire for more of the Lord in my life. I wanted to be in God's presence everyday and every time. I nearly dropped out of school in order get involved in full time ministry as I felt like school was delaying me. And in those days I did not have a car, and had to walk many times. I could sing songs of praise and worship unto the Lord, speaking in tongues as I walked on foot for many miles from place to place.

I was so sold-out to the Lord so that I was not bothered about who was around or looking at me. The most important thing was my relationship with God. I did not care about people's opinion about me– I was not ashamed of the Lord. The reason some believers cannot worship God passionately, it is because they are trying to maintain some level of dignity. (more about this in chapter 28.) You see every day; I lived with great anticipation for the second return of our Lord Jesus Christ. All I could think about was heaven; the knowing that Christ could show-up anytime, any day, and the fact that He was the very source and reason for my existence consumed my heart. I wanted everybody to hear about Jesus. I wanted everybody to get saved immediately. Others may view this as being fanatical, which I would proudly say, yes, I was indeed very enthusiastic. My prayer is that the Lord would take me back to that type of enthusiasm. As a church, we have come to a point where we are so relaxed and have become very complacent. There is no more zeal for the things of God; some of us were very fervent on fire for the Lord at some point in our lives. But today that passion has disappeared. We are absorbed with the cares of this world and the pride of life.

All we dream about is how we can make money, and agonizing all day long how we can accumulate wealth for ourselves. There is a paradigm shift in our focus towards earning ourselves recognition and fame, while losing sight of what is really most important and significant. Money and pleasure have become the hub of our lives. You used to be very committed to God. You had a very personal relationship with Jesus Christ. As a believer you were on fire for the Lord. Your thoughts were filled with the love and a desire to live for the Lord. You were always living with the expectancy of His second coming –Jesus Christ was your passion. You may still belong to some church, but you do not have that intimate, passionate, more personal relationship with the Lord.

The desire for more of the things of God is no longer there. There is no longer a hunger and thirsty for God in your life. People are neither cold nor hot, being neither too worldly, nor very spiritually committed; one can participate in the things of God, but also take part in worldly stuff as well, such as gossip, partying in clubs etc. As believers, we are trying to fit in with all people; all places, all the time; erroneously becoming all things to all men. When we are with the church people, we behave for a moment like one of them, whenever we are with those that are busy with the

158

worldly pleasures, we are there partaking of their activities and conduct as well. There is no difference between us and the unbelievers—we seem to belong to both sides, kingdoms.

God desires that we get back to the foot of the cross. He would like to take us back to the place where we first received Jesus. He wants us to "repent and do the first works", the former things. The Lord is calling us to be fully committed to Him and Him alone. He wants us to return to our first love; He says "you have left your first love". The Spirit is beckoning and calling out to you today, will you return to the Lord?

The Lord said in Matthew 5: 6 "Blessed are those who hunger and thirst for righteousness, for they shall be filled"

The Lord wants to affirm His commitment that it is the hungry and thirsty that He will satisfy; it is these that He is ready to fill. The more hungry for Him you are, the more He will fill you. It is during our dedicated moments with the Lord in worship that as we seek Him in brokenness that He will reveal Himself to us. Will you seek Him? Will you let Him ignite you with His passion once again as in days before?

◇◇◇

CHAPTER 22

DEEP CALLS UNTO DEEP

"Deep calls unto deep at the noise of your waterfalls" ~
(Psalms 42: 7).

It is truly the deep that calls to deep. It would be strange to call a doctor for someone who is well, it will be an unusual at the funeral house to comfort someone who is not bereaved or touched by the loss of a beloved. Only those that mourn shall be comforted. It is the sick who need a physician. Let me reiterate what I have said in the previous chapter that it is only the hungry that God shall fill. It is to those that are seeking Him out that He will reveal Himself.

David once said, "As the deer pants for the water brooks, so pants my soul for You, O God. My soul thirsts for God, for the living God. When shall I come and appear before God?" (Psalms 42:1–2).

It is hard to force someone to eat when they are not hungry. Such people won't know the value of the food. It will be a waste to spend your food on them. If they are forced to eat while they are already full, it will be bad for them, they may get sick, they may get constipated. If you do not know the purpose for the anointing you are likely to abuse it.

It is very easy to get water into a land which is broken or tilled. A hard and dry land will cause the water poured onto it will to slip away. Hearts which are desperately seeking out for God, passionately hungering and thirsting for God with an open heart will be filled because they are ready for spiritual rain just like the broken ground is for physical rain. These are the hearts which will be receptive to the waters of revival, the waters of the Holy Spirit of God. It is the people who say to themselves there must be more in God than this. They say to themselves there must be more in God than the ankle-deep, there must be more than the knee-deep or the waist-deep level– they desire to swim in the river of God's Spirit.

These are hearts which are always reaching out for more of God, never satisfied with mediocrity. Usually such hearts are open to rebuke, correction, and repentance, whenever they are offline in their walk with the Lord. The broken and contrite hearts the Lord will by no means cast away.

"These are hearts which are always reaching out for more of God, never satisfied with mediocrity"

Develop the hunger with the right motive.

Let us put some things in perspective here. I think the reason some people are so anointed and God has entrusted them with ministries of healing, miracles, signs and wonders is because they have grown to the level where they can be trusted to rightly and responsibly handle such anointing. They do not allow their heads to grow too big. They are not proud or pompous with desire for vain glory.

"You ask and do not receive, because you ask amiss, that you may spend it on your pleasures" ~(James 4:3).

"And do you seek great things for yourself? Do not seek them; for behold, I will bring adversity on all flesh," says the Lord. "But I will give your life to you as a prize in all places, when you go"~(Jeremiah 45:5).

We need to seek God with a pure heart and the right motive. There is nothing wrong with seeking great miracles, signs and wonders. But why do we seek those great things in our ministries. Is it just to build names, fame or our own kingdoms? In whatever you do, do you seek glory for yourself, or is it for God's glory?

God also sees the very attitude of our hearts; your attitude in life will determine your altitude. Your attitude will determine how far you will go, how much you will accomplish for God in this life. The anointing is meant to bless you and take you higher in God, and bless those who you come in contact with. But if your heart is not in the right place and you are not careful, the spirit of pride can easily creep in and you can lose it. Pride will hinder you from experiencing more of God in your life. God will not share His glory with another. We need to seek God out of a pure heart full of genuine humility.

Let us go back to our main text of Revelation 2:1-8. While God sees that we have failed and fallen short in our relationship with Him. He does not ignore or forget those times we have done well. Look at the closing verse which says, but this you have, "that you hate the deeds of the Nicolaitans, which I also hate."

I believe God wants to show us that what we do is never lost; everything we do is ever before Him. He is not unjust to forget our good works. He will reward our good works.

> "God also sees the very attitude of our hearts; your attitude in life will determine your altitude"

At the same time he highlights the areas where we have failed, so that we should not allow the good to obscure or cover the failure.

He does not want the good to deceive us into neglecting the areas where we performed poorly. In other words, there is room for change or improvement in God. When we mess up that does not mean that it is the end.

Develop the Staying-Power
God wants us to re-cultivate and rekindle that hunger and thirst we had for Him when we first gave our lives to Christ. He longs for our hearts to thirst after Him and His righteousness once again. In John 7: 37-38 the bible records;

"On the last day, that great day of the feast, Jesus stood and cried out, saying, "If anyone thirsts, let him come to Me and drink He who believes in Me, as the Scripture has said, out of his heart will flow rivers of living water"

You see Jesus is calling us right now. He longs for us to get back to our "first love". He wants us to begin to thirst and hunger for Him once again. In Luke 10:38-41 we see a typical example of the state of the church today. A church that is consumed with service, neglecting the owner of the work;

"Now it happened as they went that He entered a certain village; and a certain woman named Martha welcomed Him into her house. And she had a sister called Mary, who also sat at Jesus' feet and heard His word. But Martha was distracted with much serving, and she approached Him and said, "Lord, do you not care that my sister has left me to serve alone? Therefore, tell her to help me." And Jesus answered and said to her, "Martha, Martha, you are worried and troubled about many things. But one thing is needed, and Mary has chosen that good part, which will not be taken away from her." ~(Luke 38-42).

"They say to themselves there must be more in God than the ankle-deep, there must be more than the knee-deep or the waist-deep level– they desire to swim in the river of God's Spirit"

Service to the Lord must be balanced and should never take the place of our love for the Lord. Many times pastors, elders and deacons, preachers pray whenever there is an assignment ahead of them to fulfill. But being in the presence of God is supposed to be our way of life, not something we do when we are preparing for preaching. For Many believers worship is something they do once a week, on Sunday morning. Worship is meant to be a life-style as opposed to a 20 minute Sunday morning routine. If unchecked too much service orientation can get us too busy and so eventful that we forget to fellowship with God our Father and creator. Martha got very preoccupied with much service to the Lord. Many times we are caught up in this serving business and we neglect our fellowship and love relationship with Him. Our number one calling is not service, but fellowship with Him.

We need to reconfigure our priorities. The order must be relationship and then service. We affirm our love for Him when we spend time in His presence. And that is what Mary did. She stayed in His presence, placing intimacy before service. Our ministry must be birthed out of the relationship we have with Him. In His presence it is where we can hear His heart beat. In Isaiah 6:1-6;

"In the year that King Uzziah died, I saw the Lord sitting on a throne, high and lifted up, and the train of His robe filled the temple. Also I heard the voice of the Lord, saying: "Whom shall I send, and who will go for Us?" Then I said, "Here am I! Send me." And He said, "Go, and tell this people: `Keep on hearing, but do not understand; keep on seeing, but do not perceive. "Make the heart of this people dull, and their ears heavy, and shut their eyes; lest they see with their eyes, and hear with their ears, and understand with their heart, and return and be healed."~(Isaiah 6:1,8-10)

Isaiah saw the Lord while in His presence. This is where Isaiah received and accepted the call of God for his life. This is where God asked "Whom shall I send, and who will go for us". It is here where Isaiah got hold of the heart beat of God, the assignment for service. Ministry must be a byproduct of our relationship with God.

In the book of Acts chapter 13:1-3, we see the apostles in the church of Antioch, affirming the calling of God after spending time ministering before the Lord.

"Now in the church that was at Antioch there were certain prophets and teachers: Barnabas, Simeon who was called Niger, Lucius of Cyrene, and Manaen who had been brought up with Herod the tetrarch, and Saul. As they ministered to the Lord and fasted, the Holy Spirit said, "Now separate to Me Barnabas and Saul for the work to which I have called them.' Then, having fasted and prayed and laid hands on them, they sent them away"

As the Apostles ministered to the Lord, they heard from the Lord. They caught the heart beat of God. I believe this must have come by way of word of knowledge or prophecy in the midst of ministering to the Lord. It was in the midst of worshipping the Lord with fasting that the Lord said "Now separate to Me Barnabas and Saul for the work to which I have called them".

Oh, how I long that we learn to spend time before the Lord, just ministering, praising and worship Him. Unfortunately, the only time many believers come before God with fasting and prayer is when they are faced with a need, a difficult situation, imminent layoff at work, or when confronted with a deadly sickness that the doctors have said they cannot deal with.

I am talking about coming in His presence not to ask for stuff, but to worship Him. I pray that we will grow to a level where we will come before Him individually to worship as worshippers—where we will minister before Him, just telling him how we feel about Him, how much He means to us and declaring His greatness.

Our worship life can be a secret in our closet, but when God has anointed us, it will not be a secret. God delights in anointing our heads with oil causing our cup to run over and preparing a table in the presence of our enemies. When God blesses and lifts you up out of His holy habitation, out of His presence, it will be evident. Undisputedly everyone will know it—It will be an open secret.

Often, we come before God with our long list of prayer requests, like a grocery shopping list. We list things we want Him to give us, but rarely do we come before him with a list of the blessings and the many things He has already done, just to thank Him, Just to worship Him and tell Him much we love and adore Him. There is nothing wrong with making your requests known unto God, but let us learn to be grateful to God.

Many times we seek the blessing and not the blesser, we seek the gifts and not the giver, we seek the healing and not the healer, and we seek the comfort and not the comforter.

There is a Chinese proverb which says, "Give a man a fish and you feed him for a day; teach him how to fish and you feed him for a lifetime." So, what would you choose to be given millions of money or being taught how to make your own money?

Only a foolish man will choose fish or money, because he is shortsighted, with short-term focus. The fact is that one can eat the fish in no time and it will be gone. There are many people who won millions of dollars as lottery prize money, who ended up spending it in a flash and slipped back into poverty so quickly. They even ended up bankrupt due to lack of planning and wisdom on how to effectively manage finances. All this would have been avoided had they been taught the art of fishing or making money. If you learn the art of fishing you will always eat fish and have millions of money the rest of your life.

It is time we stopped majoring on the minors. We must start setting our priorities right. It is time to put things in the right perspective. It is time we seek the prince of peace and not just the peace. It is time we seek after God and not the gold. When we find God, we have found the gold. When we find God, we have found love, for He is Love. It is time we seek Him who is love and not just love itself.

God is the source of everything good that you will ever need in this world.

The Bible says, "for God so loved the world that He gave..." according to John 3:16. The truth of the matter is that love does not seek to receive always, but rather gives as well. What can we give to the Lord; He wants us to give Him our love our "first love" ...

Ignoring and forgetting the circumstances, the pain, heartache, difficulties and challenges. It may be the financial or marital problems you are facing right now, for a moment forget about the numerous needs that you have right now and just open your mouth loud and tell the Lord, *Lord I love you; I appreciate your love, goodness and mercy. You are Great Lord Jesus. You are so precious to me. Holy Spirit I love you. How excellent is your name in all the Earth. Receive all the Glory and Honor Lord. You are worthy Lord. Father thank you for everything you have done in my life and in the lives of my loved ones. I worship you.*

Remember the things He has brought you through, things that would have destroyed your life, the sickness which you survived when all others died. Remember the accident that killed so many others, but God's mercy saved you from it. The mighty long way He has brought you through, when others did not make it through. Can you spare a few minutes and worship Him for who He is, He is God Almighty. He is your Creator and no one can match His greatness. Please leave the book for a moment and just open your mouth and worship Him from your heart.

"It is time we seek the prince of peace and not just the peace. It is time we seek after God and not the gold. When we find God, we have found the gold. When we find God, we have found love, for He is Love"

CHAPTER 23

DEVELOP A DEEP HUNGER FOR GOD

But one thing is important- one thing is needful

In life there are things we do which are not bad or wrong in themselves, but they may just be misplaced on the ladder of priorities. We may not be doing the wrong things, but doing the right thing at the wrong time. We may also focus on what is minor instead of what is major. We may be prioritizing on the convenient instead of the significant.

Therefore, Paul in his letter to the Corinthians seeks to bring clarity regarding certain traditions such as circumcision and other ceremonial laws which believers from the Jewish background were imposing on the Gentile believers who had just come to faith in Jesus. Those traditions were slowly dividing the Church. These things were not evil and wrong in themselves, but they were not important. Here are Paul's words;

"All things are lawful to me, but all things are not expedient: all things are lawful for me, but I will not be brought under the power of any" (1 Corinthians 6:12).

Many of the good acts that we perform as believers though great as they may be, may not be absolutes in themselves. For example, good works are not absolute to Salvation, for we are saved by grace through faith. Yet faith without works is as good as dead. And while faith is important it is not an absolute by itself. That is why the Bible says that after having faith and repented of our sins, "we must go on to do works of righteousness"~(Luke 1:8). You cannot be a believer and not have a heart for the poor.

Now there are things which we concentrate on as believers more than we should. In the process we forget and leave out the most important things. There is a need for us to refocus our energies and set our priorities right. This

169

is what Jesus in Luke 10:42 is conveying to Martha when He says to her "But one thing is needful: and Mary hath chosen that good part, which shall not be taken away from her".

Mary has chosen the good part" referring to Mary's act of ministering to Jesus—sitting at His feet while Martha was busy serving tables. Although what Martha was doing was not wrong, but it was not significant at the time. Martha was service oriented while Mary was relational driven. Mary was at a place of fellowship with the Lord, while Martha was working for the Lord. It is easy to get too caught up with this as a believer as I pointed out in the preceding chapter.

My friend, God desires fellowship with us first more than anything else in the world. He longs that we seek after loving and pleasing him. He desires that we worship Him alone. In Luke 10: 42, Jesus said to Martha, "But one thing is needed, and Mary has chosen that good part, which will not be taken away from her."

I want you to see something here; Jesus our Lord does not commend Martha although she was busy trying to serve Him. When we are not careful we can concentrate on good things and forget the significant. Serving the Lord is honorable; however, it must not supersede or replace time of fellowship with Him. Our service to the Lord must stem out the love we have for our Jesus. If we love God we will desire and love to serve Him.

The word "Needed" is also translated compulsory obligatory, indispensable. The Lord is saying in Luke 10: 42' But one thing is needed, or that is 'One thing' is compulsory, obligatory. This is non-negotiable so that you cannot opt it out. It is strictly not optional; it is an obligation that we must fulfill. This is how crucial being in His presence means to the Lord. Being in the presence of the Lord must take prerogative and pre-eminence above everything else.

People can subtly get so absorbed in the church activities, like serving in the women's guild, eldership board, or whatever capacity and they can even give their money to the church; though these things are great, our service is devalued if it is done the wrong way. Service to the Lord must come out of our relationship and our love for Him. Our love must be the compelling factor.

The Weymouth's New Testament translations put it this way, "and yet only one thing is really necessary" Luke 10:42. Mary has chosen the good portion and she shall not be deprived of it"

We know very well that Jesus is more intelligent, more knowledgeable and more competent to tell us what is best. He can make the right conclusion or determination more than anybody else. Here Jesus Christ our, Master, says, "One thing is needed". In Martha's view, service was the most important thing, while Mary thinks the best is fellowshipping, sitting at the Lord's feet. There seems to be an argument, a disconnect or lack of clarity here and so the Lord comes in as the righteous judge with a final determination. He says all these things are good and great, but only one thing is needful/needed. The word "Needed" would be translated "desirable, advantageous, sought after, essential, important, vital, indispensable". Jesus is literally saying, "I desire more than anything that you sit and spend time with me" in my presence. This thing is indispensable, nothing else can replace it. It is the most important thing; nothing can match its wealth, importance or essence. I believe when Jesus says, "Only One thing," He strictly means "Only one thing" is indeed essential or important. It does not matter who says what. One can choose to hold their own opinion, but they cannot change this fact.

I think David had a foresight concerning this. He had tapped into the realm of the spirit to know and understand this issue. He makes this conclusion that only one thing was the most important in life. Be mindful that David was not an ordinary person. David had the Kingdom, rulership, all the wealth, the honor, the wives and the children, the revelations, the Psalms, the Poetry, the prophetic insights about the coming Messiah, silver and gold you can name it. He came to a steadfast conclusion where he says,

"One thing I have desired of the Lord, That will I seek: That I may dwell, in the house of the Lord all the days of my life, to behold the beauty of the Lord, And to inquire in His temple" ~ (Psalms 27:4).

David had great possession, riches and honor. No doubt he had everything one could ever dream of in life. He had experienced life in the valley, as well as life on the mountain. David had his highs and lows. He had enjoyed a lot of victories over his enemies, becoming a household name in all Israel, acclaimed and respected by all, but yet after having had and done all he concludes by saying "one thing have I desired of the Lord". In fact he says, that one thing is so important that "I will seek after". The word desired here's also translated, needed. David is therefore, saying that nothing compares to being in the House of the Lord. He says, "That I may dwell, in the house of the Lord". The house of the Lord speaks about the presence of God. It speaks of the dwelling place of God, where God is, where Jesus is, His habitation. This is where our God delights to make His home to live in as it were. In Psalms 22: 3 "But thou art holy, O thou that inhabitest the praises of Israel". That is God inhabits our praises. The house of the Lord is where the Lord lives, that is where He dwells, in Psalms 26: 8. He also says, "LORD, I love the house where you dwell, the tenting-place of your glory".

I am deeply convinced that there was something David had experienced to come to this persuasive conclusion. I believe he must have had an experience that was far greater than all the material possessions he had as a King. This is confirmed in Palms 23v 6 "Surely goodness and mercy

172

shall follow me all the days of my life; and I will dwell, in the house of the Lord Forever"

The life of a man does not consist of the things he possesses. You can have all the money there is, probably in the whole world, but you will never get contented, because man's heart never gets satisfied. Man's heart was not meant to be satisfied with stuff. There is a void that only God can fill. It is a proven fact that the more money you accumulate, the more demands are placed on you, and the more likely your expenditure pattern shifts towards your level of income.

You can own a mansion and possess a very wonderful fluffy and the most comfortable bed, but have more sleepless nights. You can have all the wealth imaginable, but never get to enjoy and know true peace. You can laugh and smile as if you are happy when you are in public, but when you stall eyeball to eyeball with reality your pillow can testify to the massive tears you shed every night.

Unfortunately, there are so many plastic smiles in the world today. True peace, I believe comes from the Lord. You will never know true peace until you find and know the Prince of Peace, Jesus Christ. This is the man who was able to sleep in the midst of the storm on the sea, when all His disciples were filled with worries, terrified and fearing for their lives—this true peace can only be found in His presence.

"But as they sailed He ~(Meaning Jesus) fell asleep. And a windstorm came down on the lake, and they were filling with water, and were in jeopardy. And they came to Him and awoke Him, saying, "Master, Master, we are perishing!" Then He arose and rebuked the wind and the raging of the water. And they ceased, and there was calm. But He said to them, "Where is your faith?" And they were afraid, and marveled, saying to one another, "Who can this be? For He commands even the winds and water, and they obey Him!" ~(Luke 8: 23-25).

173

If you can sleep in the midst of the storms, that is true peace. He was able to restfully sleep; peaceably in the midst of the storm- Therefore, he can give you peace in the midst of your life storms. He gives His beloved sleep even in the midst of chaos and confusion. The Holy Spirit will give you that kind of peace when you are so devastated with issues of life. There is righteousness, peace, and joy in the Holy Spirit.

"for the kingdom of God is not food and drink, but righteousness and peace and joy in the Holy Spirit" ~(Romans 14:17).

Peace and joy can be found only in His presence. You can have a genuine smile on your face and be happy even when you do not have money in your bank account. You can sleep like a baby even when you do not know where your next meal will come from. You too can sleep peacefully in the midst of your storm like the master. You can be at peace even when you do not know how you will pay all your bills.

Thank God, though the disciples were afraid, they knew where to turn for the answer to their problems. You can turn your storm over to the Lord. Where do you turn to when you are faced with problems in your life? Jesus is the only answer for the whole world today.

He will calm the storms raging against you. Jesus won't force it on you, or impose himself into your affairs. He is only waiting for your call. Having tried by your own means as best as you humanly know how it is time to get Him involved. It is time you look to the Lord for help.

He who calls upon the name of the Lord shall be saved. They will never be put to shame that trust in Jesus as their source of true peace. Peace like a still river will flow and joy divine will well up from deep within from the presence of God as you call upon His name and declare His greatness in your worship. . When all is said and done, when everything fails, when lights are dim and everything fades away, one thing is needed, and that is God's presence. This is the only place we will ever be when this world comes to an end.

<><><>

CHAPTER 24

THE BELIEVER'S PRIMARY CALLING

Every believer's primary calling is to be a worshipper. The only ministry given to the believer with which he can minister to God with is worship.

All other ministries and gifts are given to the body of Christ in order to equip the saints for the work of the ministry, to minister to our fellow human beings. Thus, our principal calling is to praise and worship the Lord. We are relational beings, created to relate with our maker.

In pursuant to the fact that Jesus said to Martha one thing is needful. One thing is indeed desirable, advantageous, sought after, essential, important, vital, and indispensable. When we examine the Bible in the beginning in Genesis 1:25 it says, "And God made the beast of the Earth according to its kind, cattle according to its kind, and everything that creeps on the Earth according to its kind. And God saw that it was good"

Here the Bible says, "and all that God had created was good", except that it was not complete until, Genesis 1:26 which reads, "Then God said, Let us make man in Our image, according to Our likeness; let them have dominion over the fish of the sea, over the birds of the air, and over the cattle, over all the Earth and over every creeping thing that creeps on the Earth". God created man as a relational being, capable of having a relationship with His creator.

He created man to be an extension of His rulership on Earth. God placed him in the Garden of Eden which He had planted.

Man was to exercise dominion over all of God's creation (Genesis 2:8). It was delegated and derivative authority flowing from the connection with the creator. Man was to exercise this authority in harmony and flowing out of his relationship with his creator. He was supposed to have and enjoy a close relationship. But when man sinned against God through disobedience by eating of the forbidden fruit, immediately the line of fellowship was broken as a result of that sin. And when God came to fellowship with Adam and Eve as before, they hid themselves away from His presence. This marked the advent of sin into a sinless humanity. Genesis 3:8-12:

"And they heard the sound of the Lord God walking in the garden in the cool of the day, and Adam and his wife hid themselves from the presence of the Lord God among the trees of the garden" Then the Lord God called to Adam and said to him, "Where are you?" So he said, "I heard Your voice in the garden, and I was afraid , because I was naked; and I hid myself." And He said, "Who told you that you were naked? Have you eaten from the tree of which I commanded you that you should not eat?" Then the man said, "The woman whom you gave to be with me, she gave me of the tree, and I ate."

So He drove out the man; and He placed cherubim at the east of the Garden of Eden, and a flaming sword which turned every way, to guard the way to the tree of life"

Sin will always hinder and destroy our fellowship with God. I remember growing up, whenever I had misbehaved and knew that my mother was aware of whatever I had done especially if I had defied her instructions, I did not have the courage to face her.

It was as though my line of communication with her was affected. When we are not in right standing with Him, we cannot enjoy the benefits which flow out of a wholesome relationship. Sin robs us of our authority with God; it displaces our confidence to face our own heavenly Father. It alienates us from a Holy God, which is why sinners will never enter heaven.

Sinners will never stand up to face a Holy God unless they repent and turn back to Him. Sin causes us to be unworthy to approach God's presence, because He is a

Holy God. He is too holy to behold sin. That is why Jesus cried at the cross, "why hast thou forsaken me?" The Father, for a time could not look at His only Son, Jesus who was carrying the sins of the whole world upon Himself on that cross. He became our substitution. He was bearing our sins and iniquities in His own body.

" who Himself ~(meaning Christ Jesus) bore our sins in His own body on the tree, that we, having died to sins, might live for righteousness by whose stripes you were healed" ~ (1 Peter 2: 24).

"He shall see the travail of His soul, and be satisfied. by His knowledge My righteous Servant shall justify many, for He shall bear their iniquities" ~ (Isaiah 53:11).

As a result of the original sin, all human beings are born in sin. All men are born sinners, devoid of a relationship with God. "Then the Lord saw that the wickedness of men was great in the Earth, and that every intention of the thoughts of his heart was only evil continually"(Genesis 6:5).

Consequently, man continued in rebellion and disobedience to God His creator. This has been passed on throughout all generations. Therefore, man has lived in hostility to His maker. God has always reached out to man. He has always wanted to call man back into fellowship. In the Old Testament, God gave them the law, so that, perhaps man would obey Him through observance of the law. The law failed to make man righteous by itself due to the now inherent fallen and sinful nature.

God sent His servants the prophets to teach, guide and remind His people of God's laws. But still more man fell short of God's glory and expectation of law. The institution of levitical priesthood and rituals of the various sacrifices never brought man to a level of perfection and acceptability to God, as man continued to sin against God.

179

You are called to declare His praises

The Bible in I Peter 2: 9. Says, "But you are a chosen generation, a royal priesthood, a holy nation, His own special people, THAT you may proclaim the praises of Him who called you out of darkness into His marvelous light";

The word "that" implies purpose or reason for what is said in the preceding statement. The word "THAT" has the following portrait:

'That' means 'so as to'

'That' means 'with the aim''

'That'- means 'with the purpose'

'That' - means 'with the intention'

The word 'that' in this scripture stands in to qualify or certify or rather confirm the preceding pronouncement. 'That' would therefore, render the whole scripture passage as follows;

But you are a chosen generation, a royal priesthood, a holy nation, His own special people,

"with the purpose' that you may proclaiming the praises of Him who called you out of darkness into His marvelous light; or "with the intention' that you may proclaim the praises of Him who called you out of darkness into His marvelous light"(I Peter 2 : 9).

This then means the calling of God for us out of darkness into His marvelous light was done on purpose. Therefore, our core reason God saved us is not just that we are restored to the original state, but is most importantly to place us into our rightful calling or ministry.

Even in the original state, God had created Adam for a "purpose" with an "intention" just like the manufacturer has the original intent for creating a particular product. As God's offspring, we are here for a purpose; God had an intention in creating us. Sometimes a product can have versatile uses, but it may retain its core purpose for its manufacture.

God created us to declare His praise. He created us to worship Him. He created us to fellowship with Him. This is why God used to visit Adam and Eve in the cool of the day in the Garden of Eden. The word visit speaks of fellowship, speaks of relationship. God wants to relate to us in a more personal way. He wants us to have an intimate relationship with Him.

Sacrifices of praise

As the New Testament priests according to 1 Peter 2:9, we do not have to bring sacrifices of animals such as bulls, lambs, goats and cows like the Old Testament priests did. We are called to bring to God sacrifices of praise and thanksgiving. This is our job description in the office of a priest. We are called to daily offer these sacrifices of praise from our lips; -

"Therefore, by Him Let us continually offer the sacrifice of praise to God, that is, the fruit of our lips, giving thanks to His name" (Hebrews 13:15).

Praise means, to extol, to worship, and to exalt, which also literally means to sing the praises of. We are called to proclaim, state publicly, announce, the greatness and goodness of our God. It involves our physical outward expressions such as dancing, singing with shouts of joy and jubilation, may include the use of all manner of musical instruments as we declare the greatness of our God. And worship can be done outside the parameters of the church in public such as a crusade where as believers we can openly worship the Father shamelessly, declaring what the Lord has done in our lives in the hearing of the world.

Quit Going by feelings

Praise is referred to as a sacrifice, because it is not always easy to come before God in praise and worship. When everything is fine, it is easy to abound in praise. But when life seems to fall apart, your business is going down the drain or your health is failing, offering praise becomes a sacrifice. When all things look so dark, all hope is gone, you have no money, no job and all your friends are gone because you're broke, then praise becomes very difficult to do. It is difficult to worship when the Lord seems to be distant, and after praying all manner of prayers even with fasting and there is still no answer in sight. In fact, you may have prayed and it seems like your prayers are bouncing off the ceiling back to you. It may look like God has deserted or forsaken you. And it looks like the more you pray for things to change, the worse they grow. During such moments in our walk with the Lord, offering praise can truly be a sacrifice. It is not an easy thing to do in such challenging times.

This is when we need to grow in our faith to a point where we worship God whether we feel His presence or not. We stop operating and responding to God by mere sensual feelings of our five senses. It is dangerous to go by our natural senses. They are unstable, unreliable and ever changing. Our relationship with Him must not be based our five senses. The five senses are there only to help us respond to our physical environment, but we must grow to a high level where we operate by faith, trusting in God's promises and word. Thus, whether I feel His presence or not, it does not matter. For example, my knowledge of God's love is not based on whether I feel His love or not.

Everyone must grow to the extent that their faith matures into knowledge which is far beyond outside feelings. This is where your faith rests in God's promises like this one, "behold, I will never leave you nor forsake you". This promise is not premised on how you feel. Jesus never said when you shall feel my presence, then behold I am with you. No! Of course, in our spiritual-infancy, often God allows us to experience such feelings of the closeness of His presence. But our faith must grow into knowledge. Just like Jesus when He went to raise Lazarus from the dead-a man that had been dead for four days and had started decomposing the Lord said to the Father, "I know that you hear me when I pray". Jesus our Lord might have not felt the faith at this point, but He approached the Father on the basis of the knowledge He had concerning the Father. So it does not matter whether you feel His presence or not but you know He is there with you, because He promised to be with you all the way until the end of the age.

Dear friend, realize that we are creatures of faith; learn to worship God by faith. You can worship Him by faith. I know when we are driving, crossing on a bridge for the very first-time, we do not pull over on the side to first check if the bridge is strong enough to hold us as we drive on it. But in faith we proceed to drive through the bridge without checking it out. If we can translate such faith when it comes to our walk with God, where we trust that He is always there with us in spite of our inability to sense His presence. Know that He is always there all the same, whether we sense His presence.. Let us develop such a faith in God's presence in moments of dryness and loneliness, even when we do not necessarily feel His presence.

Created to bring pleasure to God

We are called to declare God's praises; we are called to worship the King of Kings who lives forever and ever. Whenever the body of Christ comes together to lift up songs of praise to the Lord, God begins to feel good.

God's original purpose when He created all things was that everything in His creation would bring pleasure to Him "You are worthy, O Lord, to receive glory and honor and power; for You created all things, and by Your will they exist and were created"~(Revelation 4 : 11).

The King James Version –puts it this way; "Thou art worthy, O Lord, to receive glory and honor and power: for thou hast created all things, and for thy pleasure They are and were created" (Revelation 4:11).Thus,; the word

"That'- here would mean 'with the purpose of'

'That' - means 'with the intention of'

Therefore, God Himself created us as part of His creation, for Himself "with the purpose of" or 'with the intention of' bringing pleasure to His heart. And pleasure would be defined us delight, enjoyment, joy and gratification and satisfaction. It also simply means to feel good.

I believe there is nothing which brings great delight, pleasure, and satisfaction to God than, when His people begin to praise and worship Him. Worship brings delight and pleasure to the heart of our God and Father.

In most crusades where the presence of God has been super evident, it has always been where the people have focused on the Lord in unified wholehearted worship.

On many occasions, I have watched healing crusades on television with great manifestation of God's power with miracles, signs and wonders. I have often wondered "What is the secret behind such mighty manifestations?

Firstly, I believe miracles happen, because of God's mercy upon His people. This is often, expressed through the heart of compassion of the minister. Jesus during His Earthly ministry healed those who were afflicted with infirmities, demonic oppressions, and satanic bondage, as He was moved with compassion and mercy:

"Then Jesus called His disciples unto him, and said, I have compassion on the multitude, , because they continue with me now three days, and have nothing to eat: and I will not send them away fasting, lest they faint in the way" ~(Matthew 15:32).

I also believe miracles happen in the atmosphere of faith and expectancy. For sure faith is the platform for receiving miracles from God. That is when there is faith, God shows up in His power. You will remember that Jesus during His ministry life on earth told most people, "According to your faith let it be to you"

"Then He touched their eyes, saying, according to your faith let it be to you"(Matthew 9: 29).

And in Luke 17:19 it is also reported that after Jesus had healed the ten lepers and only one returned to give thanks and the Lord looked at him and said these words "Arise, go thy way: thy faith hath made thee whole" Luke 17 : 19).We also see that it was his faith that he was made whole.

Once again it is said of Jesus that He could not do so many mighty works in His hometown, because of their lack of faith or unbelief;

"And he did not many mighty works there, because of their unbelief"~(Matthew 13 : 58).(see Mark 6:5).

I believe these miracles have got something to do with one's calling and devotion to the Lord. These men have been mightily used of God because they spend quality time before the Lord. They have a personal relationship with Him. Mostly such men spend a great deal of time in God's presence in prayer and worship.

Finally, I believe worship has the ability to lift up faith in the hearts of the worshippers. As believers, lift up songs of worship to God, faith rises in their hearts. It is this faith which pleases God (Remember Hebrews 11:6). When God is pleased, delighted, He then moves and manifests His power through miracles, signs and wonders among His people.

God takes delight in our praise and worship

As God is delighted through our praise and worship, He cannot help it but come down in the midst of His people by His Holy Spirit. He manifests Himself strong and mighty on behalf of His people. He begins to minister to the needs of His people, with this is delight; He releases His mercy and heals the afflicted. You probably know how it feels when one is so delighted.

At one time when Herod was pleased and delighted with the dancing performance of the daughter of Herodias during his birthday party, he got so overtaken, and made a big promise under oath. Here's the account of this story in Matthew 14: 6-12:

"But when Herod's birthday was celebrated, the daughter of Herodias danced before them and pleased Herod. Therefore, he promised with an oath to give her whatever she might ask. So she, having been prompted by her mother, said, "Give me John the Baptist's head here on a platter." And the king was sorry; nevertheless, , because of the oaths and , because of those who sat with him at the table, he commanded it to be given to her. So he sent and had John beheaded in prison. And his head was brought on a platter and given to the girl, and she brought it to her mother. Then his disciples came and took away the body and buried it, and went and told Jesus"

In this scripture we see an earthly King so pleased and delighted with a dance to the extent of making an oath. He vowed to make good any request the daughter of Herodias would make to him. All this, because he was so delighted. He almost lost his mind and even promised her a share of his Kingdom. It is amazing to see how much one can be touched with something to his delight. The king could go so far as pledging to do anything the daughter would ask.

Do you realize that God is equally bound by His word? He has said, in His word, that none of His word will return to Him void. He has exalted His Word above His name. In other words, God will indeed honor His Word. If we can get Him delighted through our praise and worship, He will surely inhabit our praises. When He is enthroned in our praises, definitely miracles will take place. His compassion will be released as we delight and touch His heart. He will be moved with compassion and pour out His mercy upon the sick and the afflicted. There will be a greater flow and

186

release of His miracle working power and healing virtue in our midst.

This seems to explain why there has been so much manifestation of God's power in these crusades where praise and worship takes eminence. God has performed many miracles where people have totally given of themselves in worship before Him. Therefore, whenever God is delighted, satisfied, and so pleased with the worship of His people He has shown up in His power and might through miracles, signs, and wonders.

Remember Colossians 1: 16. For by Him all things were created that are in heaven and that are on earth, visible and invisible, whether thrones or dominions or principalities or powers. All things were created through Him and for Him.

And the Living Bible translation reads as follows; "Christ himself is the Creator who made everything in heaven and Earth, the things we can see and the things we cannot; the spirit world with its kings and kingdoms, its rulers and authorities; all were made by Christ for his own use and glory" (Colossians 1:16).

In Christ Jesus we are redeemed to rule and reign with Him as Kings, and as priests, to offer sacrifices of praises to our God our Father.

"And they sang a new song, saying: "You are worthy to take the scroll, and to open its seals; for You were slain, and have redeemed us to God by Your blood out of every tribe and tongue and people and nation, and have made us kings and priests to our God; and we shall reign on the Earth." ~(Revelation 5 : 9-10).

God has called us to be Kings and priests unto Himself. Yes, we are called to stand in the gap, to pray and intercede for the lost. But above all, the highest level of our calling as priests is bringing sacrifices of praise and worship unto God. Just like the daughter of Herodias was given an opportunity to reign with Herod had she chosen to ask for half of the kingdom instead of John the Baptist's head. She would have reigned with Herod. Do you understand that we are also given a similar opportunity to reign with God over principalities and powers through our praise and worship? Do you know that we exercise and execute authority over the principalities when we worship God? We operate in our God-given authority as Kings and priests. Just like earthly Kings, we too as Kings we execute vengeance and judgments written over the evil principalities and powers in the spiritual realm. (Psalms 149: 6-8).

In a world with no peace and happiness and people have no reason to be joyful, but as believers we can experience peace and joy regardless of whatever is happening in our world. As a child of God, your joy is not determined by the state of the economy. When we bring God delight through worship, we experience the joy which comes from His presence. I have experienced immeasurable joy by just being in His presence because in His presence there is fullness of joy. We have this promise in Psalms 16:11 "Thou wilt shew me the path of life: in thy presence is fullness of joy; at thy right hand there are pleasures for evermore".

◇◇◇

CHAPTER 25

WORSHIP NO HUMAN BEING

Man is a Spiritual being in need of a spiritual encounter

As reiterated at the beginning of this book, man is a spiritual being, always in need of a spiritual experience. So that man by nature longs to spiritually relate to a higher power. If man's desire to worship is misdirected he ends up worshipping things that should never be the object of our worship.

Human beings can be naturally religious. Man can worship even the most insignificant things in all creation. Foolishly, man can even make himself wooden, molten, graven images like molten calf and stoop so low as to bow down to such lifeless stuff.

It is no surprise that in the absence of the knowledge of the true God, man has often worshipped idols. Paul during one of his missionary journeys came to Greece and met the Athenians who were bound in the worship of idols. Here's the story according to Acts 17: 22-23:

"Then Paul stood in the midst of the Areopagus and said, "Men of Athens, I perceive that in all things you are very religious; "for as I was passing through and considering the objects of your worship, I even found an altar with this inscription: to the unknown God. Therefore, the One whom you worship without knowing, Him I proclaim to you:

Everything that dares to take God's place in our lives becomes an idol. An idol simply means anything that we allow to take the center-stage in our lives other than God. It is regrettable that many of us have allowed other things to take pre-eminence in our lives to the extent that those things have become idols even without us knowing. Who do you give the number one place in your life? What is it that takes God's place in your life? What is it that is standing in God's way in your life?

I know for most people it is usually certain stuff that we hold so valuable in our lives. These things which are hard to let go of even if God's Word literally says they are sinful before God. It is like we have concluded that we cannot do without such things. Man can idolize anything; it can be money, a job, material possession, celebrity, a car, a pet etc.

"Therefore, since we are the offspring of God, we ought not to think that the divine nature is like gold or silver or stone, something shaped by art and man's devising" ~(Acts 17 : 29).

Paul had to proclaim the true God, the one who must be our sore object of worship. He says to the Athenians "Him I proclaim to you: God, who made the world and everything in it, since He is Lord of heaven and Earth, does not dwell, in temples made with hands. "Nor is He worshipped with men's hands, as though He needed anything, since He gives to all life, breath, and all things" (Acts 17 : 23b-25).

It is very dangerous to make anything an idol in our lives. God will destroy anything that exalts itself above Him, and brings it to nothing. He will also bring to naught anybody who dares to defiantly occupy the throne as a god. God alone is the supreme King with all power and authority.

The man who accepts to be idolized will himself suffer loss;—it may even cost your very life if you allow people to treat you as god. And if you take the glory to yourself other than ascribing it to God, the one who deserves all the glory, you will be brought down–you will be humbled and trimmed to size.

You may be a preacher, a pastor, a President or King it does not matter what position you hold in this world. If you dare to occupy the highest seat, the seat of God, you shall end up badly. Do not assume the highest seat, because the owner of the highest seat is a jealousy God. He is a consuming fire. Do not play around with God by making yourself more highly than you ought.

Be humble rest you learn it the hard way. The people who cause you to feel so big—the people who deityfy or en-god you are putting you in danger. There is only ONE Jehovah, the Almighty God, the creator of Heaven and Earth, and the entire Universe. Allowing people to treat you as a god is a No-Go Zone! Ask Herod about the dangers of attempting to take the place of God Almighty. (Read Acts 12: 20-23).

No human being is to be worshipped
"Thou shalt have no other gods before me".~(Exodus 20:3).

It is very easy to buy into the spirit of pride especially when people praise you for what you have done and accomplished, or how anointed, how great a preacher, or singer you may be. We should always be careful when people acknowledge how good or great we are in doing something. Learn to give back all the glory to God, know that without Him we are nothing. We can do nothing without Him. Do not allow people to treat you as a god, because God has already commanded us that we shall not have any other gods beside Him (Exodus 20:3). Let us look at the experience that John had on the Island of Patmos:

"And I fell at his feet to worship him. And he said unto me, See thou do it not: I am thy fellow servant, and of thy brethren that have the testimony of Jesus: worship God: for the testimony of Jesus is the spirit of prophecy" ~(Revelation 19:10).

In this scripture we see John being overwhelmed by God's presence when an angel of the Lord appeared unto him. He is so overcome and almost worships this angel, but the angel reminds John that only God is to be worshipped.

191

So many times man by nature is so frail, weak and susceptible to worshipping some supernatural being. Man is susceptible to worship anything that seemingly surpasses man's wisdom —anything that baffles his mind or that he may view and esteem highly. He is frequently demonically enticed into worshipping fellow mortal man, or a supernatural being such as an angel. The devil is very subtle that even well meaning believers can worship fellow man without knowing — usually when we take praising or honoring of people to the extreme, especially those in authority over us. It is easy to take things too far. We are to worship no other, other than God our creator, not even angels. That is why we do not pray to angels, but to God. Angels no matter how strong, no matter their radiance, no matter how anointed or powerful they look they are servants of God and ministering Spirits to the heirs of salvation. They are never to be worshipped under any circumstance. This is why God warns us that we shall have no other gods beside Him.

Likewise, when it comes to people; never make a God out of any human being. Men of this world ought to be honored and respected, but not to be revered as gods.

No matter how great, how rich, how powerful, how popular, no matter how authoritative, compelling, no matter what their accomplishments in life may be. Many people in positions of power and influence have yielded much power and authority and have, allowed praise from people get into their heads. They feel invincible so that they have become arrogant and have accepted people to treat them as gods. They will awaken the wrath of God. This is a very hot spot. You can almost be assured you will never get away with this. You do not want to mess with God on this. This is what happened to Lucifer, now Satan. Read (Isaiah 14: 12-16, Ezekiel 28: 13-19).

Even King Nebuchadnezzar had a taste of this for seven years after he felt so accomplished. He became arrogant because of his achievements and did not give glory to God; he made himself as a god in the process. Read the story in Daniel 4:22-37. He provoked the Lord's anger as a result of his pride and arrogance. God Jehovah is the only one who is worthy of all the worship, He alone is to be worshipped.

You see God wants us to worship and honor Him as God and creator. This is why God restored the line of fellowship which was broken when Adam and Eve sinned in the Garden of Eden. My friend, He longs to fellowship with us in worship when we honor and give Him all the glory. The curtain in the temple was torn from top to bottom making a new and a living way into God's very presence. Its wall was symbolic of our alienation from God as a consequence of sin. Sin had become a wall of partition which kept us in seclusion from God. We are now made accepted into the beloved. A truly loving father will stop at nothing in trying to mend bridges with his son just to reinstate the line of fellowship. Our heavenly Father did exactly that while we were yet sinners; He spared not His dear son, but gave Him up as a sacrifice to bring many sons into His Kingdom, "He who did not spare His own Son, but delivered Him up for us all, how He not with Him shall also freely give us all things?"(Romans 8: 32).

Now we can worship Him and Him alone; for He alone is worthy and greatly to be praised in all the Earth.

<><><>

CHAPTER 26

PATHWAY INTO HIS PRESENCE

There is a pathway into the presence of God that we all need to understand if we are to truly enter in and enjoy being in the Lord's presence. You know God is great. He is the King of Kings and Lord of Lords.

It takes a defined protocol to get before an earthly King or President. Most of the things that happen here on earth are only a replica or parallel to that which is in the spiritual realm. Just like you cannot just shabbily and scruffily walk before the King since there is a dressing which is considered appropriate and respectful.

And so is God worthy of all the respect. Many of us if we are called to have an audience with our national President, we would get so busy with so much preparation. I am sure some of us will go shopping for new formal clothes, possibly a nice suit, shoes, some cologne —we would most likely work on our hair; getting a nice hair cut or hair-do.

We can do all this just to make sure we look our best, appropriate, and presentable before an earthly President or King. This is exactly what happened when the King of Persia called for a beauty contest throughout his Kingdom in order to choose for himself a queen who would become his wife. Let us read the story in the book of Esther 2: 1-17:

"......"and let the king appoint officers in all the provinces of his kingdom, that they may gather all the beautiful young virgins to Shushan the citadel, into the women's quarters, under the custody of Hegai the king's eunuch, custodian of the women. And let beauty preparations be given them. And Mordecai had brought up Hadassah, that is, Esther, his uncle's daughter, for she had neither father nor mother. The young woman was lovely and beautiful. When her father and mother died, Mordecai took her as his own daughter...Now the young woman pleased him, and she obtained his favor; so he readily gave beauty preparations to her, besides her allowance. Then seven choice maidservants were provided for her from the king's palace, and he moved her and her maidservants to the best place in the house of the women... Each young woman's turn came to go in to King Ahasuerus after she had completed twelve months' preparation, according to the regulations for the women, for thus, were the days of their preparation apportioned: six months with oil of myrrh, and six months with perfumes and preparations for beautifying women.......And Esther obtained favor in the sight of all who saw her... The king loved Esther more than all the other women, and she obtained grace and favor in his sight more than all the virgins; so he set the royal crown upon her head and made her queen instead, of Vashti" ~(Esther 2: 3,7,9,12,17).

There is a need for preparation;

In the book of Esther as outlined above scripture, before all the young beautiful ladies could appear before the King, they had to undergo a strict preparation according to specific regulations. This preparation had to go on for a period of twelve months.

If you are invited to meet the head of state or President, There is always a need for you to make preparation which may take various forms.

Often such preparation may include training in protocols and etiquette of how to behave before the King or President. The protocol or code of behavior for instance, may require you not to walk into the Presidential suite to meet him anytime unless you are told to do so at set times.

You cannot just walk scruffily before the King with your shirt out or untucked or with your hands in the pockets. You do not appear before the King chewing gum in your mouth, as this would be childish and disrespectful.

I remember each time we had our nation's head of state attending our church annual conferences, we would have rehearsals usually a day or two prior to his coming. A team of state officials who specializes in presidential detail and security would brief us on protocol of government or Presidential function. They would drill us for example, on how we were supposed to move to the podium. You are not allowed to walk about before the head of state while he was seated. You are not allowed to pick your pockets before the President as a security measure and as a matter of respect to the office. You may agree or not with some of these so-called protocol or etiquette for earthly leaders. You may not like the President but it is demanded of you to respect him by virtue of his office. I believe some of these things are a parallel of the heavenly things.

There is a spiritual protocol for us to follow when it comes to coming into the presence of the King of Kings and Lord of Lords, our master and creator, our heavenly Father that we must be acquainted with.

Inevitability it requires us to prepare ourselves by setting aside time to sanctify our lives before we come to minister to the Lord. This is why it is so vitally important for worship leaders and worship teams or ministers that they learn to have special preparatory time.

Our spirits need preparation

We need to understand as a church that praise and worship is a progression. It is a walk of life, which does not begin when we get in the church, but it is supposed to be a continuation of where we left-off when we left home. This is also significantly the reason we ought to live in the home as believers just like we want to portray when we are in church. You should live as a Christian while in the church as well as in the community. Wherever you are, represent Christ in all your conduct even in the absence of other fellow church members.

True Christianity is how we conduct ourselves in the private, when no other human being is seeing us. Can our family members honestly bear witness that we are truly Christians? Home is where our true self is exhibited. It is so easy to say it is ok to a brother or sister in the Lord when they step on our toes in church. It is so simple to put up a good show, to pretend, or hide our real feelings before our church folks so we can look good while our very hearts cannot bear witness to our speech.

This is why Paul told the believers in Philippi saying in Philippians 2 : 12 "Wherefore, my beloved, as ye have always obeyed, not as in my presence only, but now much more in my absence; work out your own salvation with fear and trembling"

Many people have a propensity to live a godly life before their pastor or church leaders in a bid to win their favor and commendation. But what is important is to win God's approval and favor. Do not be a men pleaser but rather choose to glorify God at all times in spite of who is or is not there with you.

You may hide from people but you can never hide away from God. He can see what you do in the very darkest night, and even though the darkness hides you for darkness is as light before Him.

"whither shall I go from thy spirit? or whither shall I flee from thy presence? If I ascend up into heaven, thou art there: if I make my bed in hell, behold, thou art there. If I take the wings of the morning, and dwell, in the uttermost parts of the sea" ~(Psalms 139:7-9).

You cannot fool around and expect to come in church the next morning and put up a show before the Lord. We must consecrate our lives on a daily basis even before we appear before the presence of the Lord. Prepare your heart and life personally before appearing in His presence.

Deal with past and present Sin and guilt.

We need to watch the conduct of our lives before coming to worship the Lord. If we know there is any sin in our lives we ought to come before the Lord in humility to confess, repent and ask God for His forgiveness. This will help us to have the liberty to enter in and enjoy the presence of the Lord.

Remember the devil is the accuser of the brethren. Revelation 12:10, records, "Then I heard a loud voice saying in heaven, "Now salvation, and strength, and the kingdom of our God, and the power of His Christ have come, for the accuser of our brethren, who accused them before our God day and night, has been cast down"

Understand that condemnation and convictions are totally two different things. The Holy Spirit is the one who brings conviction of sin upon the heart of a believer. He does this in order to bring us to a place of repentance, to restore us to a sweet fellowship with our God. Bear in mind, sin if not dealt with will always stand in the way of our fellowship with our heavenly Father. On the other hand, condemnation never comes from God but from the devil. Satan will do this to disapprove and make us feel so unworthy to come before God. The devil's goal is to make you feel like a dirty piece of junk when you come before God. This is why He is called the accuser of the brethren; he never stops to bring accusations about our shortcomings before God.

"And I heard a loud voice saying in heaven, now is come salvation, and strength, and the kingdom of our God, and the power of His Christ: for the accuser of our brethren is cast down, which accused them before our God day and night"(Revelation 12:10).

Always be reminded that we are made righteous not, because of the good deeds. We do not work to earn acceptance before God. Our works do not make us righteous; they are as filthy rags before Him (Isaiah 64:6).

199

It is Christ's righteousness which makes us acceptable before God. And once we are made righteous, we do not lose that right standing with God when we stumble and fall— lest Christ would have had to die over and over again each time we failed. This is, because Jesus already paid the price for our righteousness. However we have work to do, to grow in that righteousness into holiness.

Satan tries to hold us in the past; in our past failures and sins. The devil shamelessly attempts to make you feel guilty of a sin which you have already confessed and repented. If the devil can do that with a sin which has already been repented of, what more with an unconfessed and unrepented sin. He will always remind you of the sin you committed yesterday. When the devil reminds you of your past sin you can as well, remind him of his defeat 2000-years ago which is still in force to date and forever. Once more, you can as well remind the devil of his future that he is doomed forever— he can never and will never get saved or forgiven, and he shall be thrown into the lake of fire, which is already prepared for him and his angels.(Matthew 25 : 41). The devil will always tell you that you are the worst sinner who does not deserve to come near God. He will try to do this whenever you try to enter into God's presence. He does not stop to accuse the brethren before God day and night. Often such condemnation will be strong when you want to praise and worship God.

If you have confessed that sin, know for sure that God has forgiven you and cleansed you. He has forgiven you and forgotten it; you have this promise in Isaiah 43 : 25 "I, even I, am He who blots out your transgressions for my own sake; and I will not remember your sins. He does not hold you in guilt anymore. This is also affirmed in Romans 8: 1, "There is therefore, now no condemnation to those who are in Christ Jesus, who do not walk according to the flesh, but according to the Spirit"

You can now come into His presence with a clear conscious without guilt or fear with all confidence knowing that you have been made acceptable in the beloved.

God has "predestined us to adoption as sons by Jesus Christ to Himself, according to the good pleasure of His will, to the praise of the glory of His grace, by which He has made us accepted in the Beloved" (Ephesians 1 : 5-7).

Thus, it can never be God, the Holy Spirit bringing condemnation as a conviction once we have repented of any sin. The Holy Spirit will convict us in love to bring us before the Lord in repentance. The Holy Spirit neither condemns us when we sin nor does He convict us any more after we have genuinely repented a sin. Once all sin is confessed and repented of, it is buried under the blood of Jesus. For "If we confess our sins, He is faithful and just to forgive us our sins and to cleanse us from all unrighteousness" (1 John 1 : 9). Consequently, we have a responsibility to stay away from that sin which so easily beset us.

You need to know that you do not need to carry a load of guilt in your heart once you have confessed that sin. For whatever God has cleansed no one, not even the devil, is to call it unholy or uncommon. Now do not beat yourself, learn to forgive yourself and move on.

In Acts 10: 1-16, Paul was told four times in this vision to arise, kill, and eat the so-called unclean animals. These animals were regarded as unclean, unholy, according to Jewish customs in the old covenant. But God told him to rise up, kill and eat them. This was to prove and confirm to him that "whatever God has cleansed do not call uncommon" What God has cleansed let no man, not even the devil call uncommon, unclean or unholy. The devil cannot and should not call you unclean or unholy once you have been declared clean by God's Word. You can shout it out loud; I am holy, sanctified by the blood of Jesus Christ. I am the righteousness of God in Christ!"

201

Jesus said you are now clean by the word which I have spoken to you (John 15:3). "Who shall bring a charge against God's elect? It is God who justifies, who then can condemn us if God has declared us clean?"(Romans 8: 33-34.)

Once we have established ourselves on this ground, only then can we have the confidence and boldness to come into God's presence in worship without any guilt.

Deal with all unforgiveness

All the unforgiveness and grudges which we hold against people who have wronged us can equally be as bad as sin itself. There is no excuse for holding anyone in our hearts. We may try to justify ourselves for our actions. You may feel justified to carry that bitterness and may feel like you have the right to do so, but there is no validation scripturally for that. Whether we were unjustly offended or not, we have no right whatsoever to keep any grudges. We have to release those who have offended us.

Matthews 5: 23 -24 the Lord tells us, "Therefore, if you bring your gift to the altar, and there remember 'that your brother has something against you, "leave your gift there before the altar, and go your way. First be reconciled to your brother, and then come and offer your gift"

The Altar speaks of a place of sacrifice. Our praise and worship is a sacrifice before God in the new covenant. If you recall that you need to clear out some outstanding issues with somebody, it is absolutely necessary to have those things sorted out, so that they do not become a hindrance to your sacrifice before God.

I wonder how many of our sacrifices of praise have been acceptable to God. It can be in family feud, or in a relationship between husband and wife that they may not be in good terms, holding grudges against each other, but yet standing with hands lifted to Lord having unresolved issues between them —such sacrifices will not be acceptable to God. Jesus when talking to His disciples regarding the offenses we face from time to time in Luke 17:1-4:

"Then He said to the disciples, "It is impossible that no offenses should come, but woe to him through whom they do come! "It would be better for him if a millstone were hung around his neck, and he were thrown into the sea, than that he should offend one of these little ones. "Take heed to yourselves. If your brother sins against you, rebuke him; and if he repents, forgive him. "And if he sins against you seven times in a day, and seven times in a day returns to you, saying, `I repent,' you shall forgive him.'

The Lord says it is absolutely impossible that no offences should come our way. What matters is how we respond to the offences whenever they come our way. Are we going to allow unforgiveness to master our lives? There is a great price that both, the offended and the offender pays if these are not dealt with promptly. It is been reported that unforgiveness causes certain chemicals to be released into the body which may have negative effects on one's well being. In particular, it is reported that unforgiveness may bring about heart problem and stomach ulcers. It is more deadly, more poisonous than you think. You may have a lot to lose than gain in the long-run. Will you allow this to go on?

So we are faced with a choice between accepting to forgive others, release them and get on with life or hold on tightly to grudges and let them eat us up from the inside out. We may pretend for a season. It may appear fine for a season but seasons do not last forever, soon it shall be revealed. Now is the best time to deal with all bitterness, anger, unforgivenesss and resentment you have harbored so long. You may have to swallow your pride and humble yourself in reaching out to the one you are holding in your heart, forgive and ask them to forgive you as well. God is

203

so amazingly going to heal all the heartache and pain you have carried for so long.

Let us create an atmosphere conducive for the supernatural, where God can manifest Himself to us by keeping our relationships in order. The Bible says we must live peaceably with all men "Pursue peace with all men, and holiness, without which no one will see the Lord" (Hebrews 12:14).

God knows that it is possible to be at peace with all men. He will never ask us to do something that we are incapable of doing. When you have released and forgiven those people you had held as captives in your heart for so long, you will be free yourself. This will help you personally to have the liberty as you come before the Lord in worship. If we can relate well with fellow brothers and sisters, then we can also relate well with God. Then we can love God in truth. praise and worship is an expression of our love to the Lord. If we love God we will love all men without any prejudice or resentment.

<><><>

CHAPTER 27

GETTING INTO THE VERY PRESENCE OF GOD

As indicated at the beginning of the preceding chapter, as believers we also need to understand that praise and worship has a progression, which must be followed if we are to enter.

At the beginning of every worship session, everyone begins in the flesh—we are self-aware, self- conscious and so connected to our environment. Our minds may be wondering and occupied with many things, cares and concerns of life. And so it is not easy to break through the clutter as we struggle to focus on the Lord. We may be more thrilled with music and feel good and enjoy the praise, but not necessarily enter in. Let us take a close look at this scripture;

"Enter into His gates with thanksgiving, And into His courts with praise. Be thankful to Him, and bless His name"~(Psalms 100: 4).

This verse seems to suggest to us that there is a house that we are trying to enter in. It looks very much like a palace or a mansion which has a gate all around.

In the old days before anyone could have an audience with the King they had to pass through some seclusion barriers, which were called palace-gates. These were usually big gates or doors that were firmly secured. Most ancient cities were closely shut in with high, big walls for protection from enemy invasion. The words 'enter' is originally translated from the Hebrew word bo' which means 'to go' or 'come' - abide, in, into, to pass, to come in, out, upon, to pass, enter ~(in, into,-tering, -trance,

There is a way of entrance into His presence which every believer must learn and understand in order to effectively worship the Lord. Unfortunately, many times well meaning children of God do not enter-in, they do not breakthrough into the very realm of deep, intimate, heart-to-heart worship. Let us closely look at the way of entrance into the very presence of God:

Thanksgiving takes us into the holy place

In summary, the presence of God is like a city or house that must be entered by passing through some kind of gates. For us to get in we must get access through some kind of a door just like one requires a key in order to enter in a home. We are called upon to find the access code into His presence. Thanksgiving works as the key for access into the presence of God. It opens the gates into the heavenly places, into the presence of God. When we lift up our voices in thanks to God, we open for ourselves a way into that holy place.

The tabernacle of David had three segments, namely the 'outer court', 'holy place', and the most Holy place called 'the holies of holies', praise takes place in his courts and worship takes us into the very inner most, holy place where we can encounter the Lord.

Now remember thanksgiving takes us through these outer most gates into the outer court into the presence of God. In the Old Testament days, most cities and kings palaces were secured from enemy invasion by building huge wall around it. And before you could get into the palace to meet the King, you had to pass through some gates and security personal. Even today, you cannot just get to the president say at the White House directly; you have to pass through the gate and so much security in order to reach the President.

The same thing goes with company executives. If you have an appointment to meet the most senior person of a corporation such as a company president or CEO, normally you have to pass through several checkpoints, security personnel, and secretary before meeting the executive. Most cases security personnel can ask you many questions as a matter of security protocol. They may look at you to see if your appearance is befitting for you to meet such a high ranking person.. Sadly, many people are turned away or denied entry into some of these premises even right from the outer gate by the security personnel based on mere appearance.

Please understand that Christ has opened the way for us to get into God's presence through his own body, remember the curtain of the temple was torn from top to bottom at the time of his death. This signified the fact that we have the authority to come into God's presence through Jesus Christ our Lord. You will never be turned away. No one can question you or stop you from coming before your heavenly father, not even the devil can stop you.

No guilt, shame or past sin should discourage you from coming into the presence of God. As long as you have repented and given your life to Jesus, you are entitled to have access before God. Only you can hinder yourself access into the presence of God. You must break free from the flesh and everything that would potentially hinder you from entering into the very presence of God.

We can draw some lessons, if men of this world are held in high respect and require protocol to meet them, there is a spiritual parallel. Just like one cannot walk before these people in senior or executive positions callously, there is need for a proper and modest way of dressing when we come before the Lord. And more than that there is need for the appropriate dressing of our hearts before God, the adorning of the inward man (1 Timothy 2:9-10, Colossians 3:10-12). You have been clothed in God's righteousness because Christ has become our righteousness.

God is above all the earthly rulers and authority, regardless of the position or the title. God is the supreme ruler of the whole universe. r. All authority has to bow to the authority of God. Every knee must bow at the mention of the name Jesus, and every tongue confesses that He is Lord.

Praise ushers us into the holy Places

Again in reference to our scripture from Psalms 100:4;

"Enter into His gates with thanksgiving, And into His courts with praise. Be thankful to Him, and bless His name".

In Hebrew the word courts is the word khaw-tsare' and in its original sense; it would mean yard (as enclosed by a fence); also a hamlet ~(as similarly surrounded with walls): - court, tower, village.

NOW since we have already passed through the gates, by our thanksgiving, we come into this place called the outer courts.

It is not easy to pass through the outer court into the holy place. While almost everybody can pass through the outer gates through thanksgiving into the outer court on their way into the presence of God, There is always something that we can recall, things the Lord has done for us in our individual lives. It is the time when the whole church can rise-up with thanksgiving or praise songs; everybody can declare what God has done for them and thank Him. At this point corporate worship takes place and everybody can jump, shout and dance to all the praise songs. Even sinners can participate and walk in and out of the church without any change or transformation; they leave the church the same way they came in. It is at the outer court where everybody easily participates and enjoys all the fun and the entertainment.

In the Hebrew the word here for praise and thanksgiving is Teh-hil-law' which refers to the praises and thanksgiving that goes with laudation; specifically (concretely) by a hymn, or chant, song: praise.

I am sorry to say that most churches these days have become the entertainment centers in town, serving the

208

similar interests like Hollywood celebrities— whose occupation is nothing other than entertaining the world.

It is as if the world can come into the church and is trying to influence the church. If we are not careful here's where the church can lose its savor and become like the world. This is where Paul would have called the church by the mercies of God, to no conform themselves to the world. (Romans 12:2). I truly believe the church must be exciting, praise must be wonderful, and professional, but all must be done with modesty, genuinity in spirit and in truth. We can make the people to sweat with dancing as they get entertained in the church as much as we want, but we must look for the lasting, eternal impact—a mark that we leave in the lives of all we interact with after all the entertainment and excitement has faded away. We must deeply yearn for transformation of our lives as we worship God. We must long for something deeper than mere entertainment, an impact which goes beyond mere fun in the church.

The very last portion of this scripture "Be thankful to Him''. In the original Hebrew it is the word Yadah used only as denotative from literal meaning to use (that is, hold out) the hand; physically to throw at or away; especially to revere or worship with extended hands;

This is a strong call to go a little yonder. That is where we go beyond the mere stamping of feet in dance as most African-Americans do, twisting the whole body like the Africans do or jumping as most of our white brothers do, but our worship includes the lifting of the hands as well. Thus, physically throwing out or extending of hands in a more deeper and serious worship level.

This is the very beginning of us moving from more physical display of praise and thanksgiving to a much deeper, focused, and surrender to God in worship.

At this point we begin to die to our natural surroundings. The lifting of the hands speaks of surrender. Thus we say to the Lord, 'we are no longer in charge, but we surrender to you'. We humble ourselves before the Lord. Here we do not mind about who is looking at us—we cease to do stuff just to impress somebody with our dance and styles. This takes us out of the outer court into the holy place.

We start to tell God what He means to us. We cease to thank God with a thought at the back of our minds which ascribes all blessing to our credit. As believers we grow in God's grace—we do not think of ourselves as more deserving than others. It is not an unusual for us to get tempted into thinking that we got blessed because of what we did for God, but this is where we do not think like that.

It is where there is less of us, but more of Him. It ceases to be all about me...me...me..., but Him and Him alone. We begin to a scribe all the glory to Him who sits on the throne. This is where the real praise begins to transition to worship. Where we begin to enter into the most holy place, the holy of holies

◇◇◇

CHAPTER 28

WORSHIP AS THOUGH DEAD

"Enter into His gates with thanksgiving, and into His courts with praise: be thankful unto him, and bless His name"~ (Psalms 100:4).

The very last portion of the above scriptures says "be thankful unto him, and bless His name" In Hebrew the word "bless" is Barak.

And this word barak is strongly translated to kneel ~ (down); by implication it literally means to bless God as an act of adoration, and congratulate, or praise, salute.

This place is where man must completely die to self. This is where we completely forget about who we are in society. It is the time when we become like children before our heavenly Father.

This is the highest form of praise and adoration, which is called worship. Here we begin to prostrate before God. We forget who we are in the eyes of all people. All that we care about is that God would be glorified. We adore, and bow our knees before the Lord to honor Him.

This looks like what happened to Saul while he was on the road to Damascus. Suddenly, he encountered the Lord Jesus Christ in person. And a total transformation took place in the life of Saul as a result of this unusual encounter with the Lord. He came to know Jesus as Lord, as he fell to the ground; he realized that this man who threw him off his horse must surely be above him. This made Him realize that this was no mere man. This man was surely greater than him and he immediately calls him LORD. Just as when you are flying in an airplane, the higher you go, the smaller and smaller the things get on the Earth until you can see them no more. The things on the ground cease to matter anymore. Likewise when we are caught up in the spirit of worship everything on the ground becomes nothing, but shadows in the light of His presence. At this point, the reason we live, or breath is to worship Him. The reason we are bothered and are anxious about everything is because we have not learned this secret.

Dear friend, the higher-up we go in worship before the Lord, the more our challenges and problems will diminish and become nothing and they will be as nothing. We will not even mind our highest achievements, which at times tend to hold us back from freely expressing our worship to the Lord. We feel too important, too dignified to kneel down before the Lord in worship in the church when we consider our status in society.

You may be on your own horse of achievements, accomplishments, and success; you may have a great name, or fame in society and all over the world, but when it comes to this encounter those things become as dung, they become nothing. And Christ becomes everything, all in all, supreme authority; Jesus Christ becomes Lord over all. This is where we worship God on a more intimate and personal way.

The glory revealed causes us to see Jesus as Lord

Saul, who would later become the great Apostle Paul, could not remain the same having encountered the Lord Jesus in His glory. When that bright light shone on him, it made him temporarily blind, so that he had to be led by somebody as a blind person into the city. The Jesus Christ, whom he had just acknowledged was indeed Lord and was humbling him.

Being on a horse, (the horse speaks of strength and authority.) Saul was an authority among the Pharisees; he certainly realized that the one who made him fall from his horse to the ground must have been greater than himself. In recognition and acceptance of this fact he instantly acknowledged by addressing Jesus Christ as Lord, "who are you Lord?"

I know at some point, we are overtaken by pride and we may think of ourselves more highly than we ought. Thinking we are where we are by our strength or intelligence or education. We esteem ourselves too highly and inappropriately so that we want to come before God as if He were the created, instead of approaching Him with all reverence Creator.

If men deserve honor and respect what more with our God who is the creator of the whole world. Men of this world ought to be honored and respected, but they are not to be revered or worshipped as gods. It does not matter how great, rich, powerful, or popular they may be—no human being is to be worshipped.

Worship Him As though Dead

John in the book of Revelation 1:16-17 writes about the experience he had while on the Island of Patmos. He says that when he saw Jesus in His glory, he could not stand it.

"And he had in His right hand seven stars; and out of His mouth went a sharp two-edged sword and His countenance was as the sun shineth in His strength"

"And when I saw him, I fell at His feet as dead. And he laid His right hand upon me, saying unto me, Fear not; am the first and the last:" ~ (Revelation 1:16-17).

Apostle John says when he saw the glory of our Lord Jesus in his strength and power; he could not stand but fell down to the ground. This would explain the reason when the presence of God, the anointing of God is strong upon people some fall to the ground, because these mortal bodies cannot stand it. This is referred to as being slain in the spirit. He fell down to the ground as a result of this encounter with the risen Lord.

Whenever we get into contact with the very presence of God oftentimes cannot stay on our two feet. These bodies cannot just take it. I have seen even preachers while

213

preaching fail to stand by themselves because of the intensity of the glory of God. Many of them fall to the ground as a result of the magnitude of the glory of God.

When God manifests himself to us we cannot remain the same. Our lives will be changed and totally transformed. Do not tell me you had an encounter with God if your life is still the same as it was ten years ago –no real change.

We must learn to come before God in all humility and brokenness of heart, for a broken and contrite spirit He will not despise "The sacrifices of God are a broken spirit: a broken and a contrite heart, O God, thou wilt not despise" (Psalms 51:17).

The word contrite in the original Hebrew is the word dakah which means to- collapse thus, physically or mentally, as though dead. Thus, it is similar to what John experienced here. He fell down as though dead, yet he was still alive. Only that his mental and physical being became as though collapsed. Many times we come before God full of ourselves, full of what we think we are. As indicated earlier we need to learn to die to self. It does not matter how affluent or famous we may be. It does not matter what our accomplishments may be, but whenever we are before God in worship we must die to all that and focus on the Lord. We empty of ourselves, of all the pride and come in humility.

As a worship leader, I have seen people during worship desire to kneel down and worship God, but they hold back when they consider their expensive apparel, their makeup and hair-do or people around them.

We must learn to be children when we come before our heavenly Father. Jesus also said that if we are to enter heaven, we must receive the kingdom as the little children, "Verily I say unto you, whosoever, shall not receive the kingdom of God as a little child shall in no wise enter therein" (Luke 18:17).

There is something very special with the way children behave. Little children are so innocent, they are very selfless. They are never bothered with people's opinion unlike adults–we get overly concerned about what people will say. We rationalize things too much and pretend to be so disciplined, so that we are enslaved thereby. Children are able to freely express their feelings, be it about their parents or something they may be experiencing at the time. When they are happy they will express it. They will express it by dancing, singing, laughing, jumping or clapping or running all over the place. When they are sad or disappointed they will not fake it, but express it clearly as well. They rarely pretend about stuff.

As children of God we are supposed to be free before our heavenly Father. It is alright to prostrate on the floor in the presence of God. God is not ashamed of us when we freely express the way we feel while in His presence; you can be free to dance yourself out, laugh, or even cry before Him in humility and adoration. God does not get agitated or disturbed when we're just ourselves before Him as we worship Him. It does not inconvenience God when we cry or shout as you worship Him – you can go ahead and do it so long it is done in reverence of Him. He will never have a nervous breakdown. If you feel like laughing in the spirit just go ahead and do it. We are supposed to learn to express ourselves freely before God our Father. Learn to liberate yourself in the presence of your heavenly dad; do not inhibit or suppress your feelings as they bubble inside your heart during worship.

The most beautiful thing is that the Holy Ghost is not domineering or controlling, we can still retain our sanity and wisdom even after worshipping Him. God has not given us the spirit of fear, but of love, and a sound mind, we have a sound mind. It is okay to be fanatical before the Lord. After being fanatical before the presence of God for a season we can wake up and face the real world, as real people with wisdom and intelligence. You can humbly and reverently kneel down, dance, prostrate before God in worship whether you are CEO, General Manager, or Managing Director, or President. Because after you get up you will still be a manager at your workplace and perform even better as you will now be full of the presence of God.

If the world can get so fanatical, over-enthusiastic as sports fans or a celebrity to the extent of taking off their shirts, painting their whole bodies with their team's colors or flag. What about getting sold-out to God? It is time to get radical about our love for the Lord. We can worship God without any apologies or reservations whether you live in the White House, the Sanjika palace or Birmingham Castle, or the ghetto. It is time to worship God without reservations.

Bless the Lord with all that you are

God created us with integrated emotions and sensations. Man is made up of the spirit, soul and the body. The body comprises the brain and the five senses, the soul compasses the mind, the intellect and emotions, and the Spirit is the real person, the part of man which connects with the spiritual realm. Matthew 22:37 "Jesus said unto him, Thou shalt love the Lord thy God with all thy heart, and with all thy soul, and with all thy mind"

My dear friend, worship the Lord with everything that you are. Everything within us is to worship the Lord. David said, "Bless the LORD, O my soul: and all that is within me, bless His holy name" (Psalms 103:1).

This level of worship is where we die to the pride of life and high self esteem. It is where we are so real, open and humble before God. We become so broken and totally sold-out to the Lord. We are not bothered by what people say about us as long as what we are doing pleases our heavenly Father. If it is to sing before the Lord in worship, you sing your lungs out– never worried about how bad or cracked your voice sounds. You sing as unto the Lord. If it is to dance, you do it without being ashamed of people. You can abase yourself in reverence and worship to God without reservations.

The man after God's own Heart

I used to wonder why David is called a man after God's own heart, yet when you closely examine his life you will see some shortcomings. It is apparent that although he was a great King, a great fighter who fought and won so many fierce battles, yet he is the man who also made many blunders or mistakes. He is the man who also committed what we would consider as grave sins in our days.

You will see that although David had his own wife, he gave in to lust for more women and ended up marrying so many more wives. He also committed multiple sins in sequence. He miserably gave in to the spirit of lust, committing adultery with Uriah's wife. Consequently, in an attempt to cover up his sin or in modern day English; he tried to destroy the evidence by wickedly formulating a plan to eliminate Uriah by placed him in the fiercest battle front in order to have him killed by the enemy soldiers. In the end, he did not just commit adultery, but also committed murder of an innocent man. You can read the full story in 2 Samuel 11: 1-27.

Yet, despite his sinful history and inadequacy, he is at the core of the lineage of Jesus Christ. He is also called the man after God's own heart. In fact Jesus is referred to as "the Son of David" as one of Lord's royal titles. How is this possible for an individual whose life was not perfect that the son of God, the one who lived blameless among sinful men, but yet without sin should come through his lineage? This prompted my study about what it is that made David that unique.

In studying the life of David, I have discovered certain aspects of his life that are profound. There are so many other good things about David that we cannot exhaust to share right here. However, let me draw your attention to some of these things concerning the life of David.

"He was broken and so open to rebuke and correction" ~ (2 Samuel 12: 1-31).

"He was so sensitive to God and the prophetic in His life" ~ (1 Chronicles 25: 1)

"He even prophesied about the coming Messiah" ~ (Psalms 2: 1-7), (Psalms s 16: 8-11).

"He respected the anointing and the anointed of the Lord" ~ (1 Samuel 24: 4-10).

"He was so humble, so contrite before the Lord" ~ (Psalms 51: 1-19), (I Samuel 6: 16-22).

Now Let us talk a little bit regarding the last point which is relevant to our subject on praise and worship. Sorry I will include a lengthy passage of scripture for us to consider. In the following scripture we see David as King of Israel in a worship procession as they bring the Ark of God into the City of David.

"And David danced before the LORD with all his might; and David was girded with a linen ephod. So David and all the house of Israel brought up the ark of the LORD with shouting, and with the sound of the trumpet. And as the ark of the LORD came into the city of David, Michal Saul's daughter looked through a window, and saw King David leaping and dancing9 before the LORD; and she despised him in her heart. And they brought in the ark of the LORD, and set it in his place, in the midst of the tabernacle that David had pitched for it: and David offered burnt offerings and peace offerings before the LORD. And as soon as David had made an end of offering burnt offerings and peace offerings, he blessed the people in the name of the LORD of hosts.... Then David returned to bless his household. And Michal the daughter of Saul came out to meet David, and said, how glorious was the king of Israel today, who uncovered himself today in the eyes of

218

the handmaids of his servants, as one of the vain fellows shamelessly uncovereth himself! And David said unto Michal, It was before the LORD, which chose me before thy father, and before all, his house, to appoint me ruler over the people of the LORD, over Israel: Therefore, will I play before the LORD. And I will yet be vile than thus, and will be base in mine own sight: and of the maidservants which thou hast spoken of, of them shall I be had in honor. Therefore, Michal the daughter of Saul had no child unto the day of her death. ~ (2 Samuel 6:14-23).

Although David was a King, but when it comes to praising and worshipping God, he was ready to be a child before his heavenly Father. His position in the society did not dictate how much he danced; his dignity or royalty was nothing. He would forget himself and just focus on God in His presence. This is what dying to self is all about; all about you becomes nothing, but all about him, and him alone. That is when you do not allow your position or status to come in the way of your relationship with God. This is also-called, worshipping God as though dead. The dead are not influenced by what is around them. I have seen no matter how hard the bereaved mourn at a funeral, the dead one is just as dead as ever. The dead one is not bothered at all. They are not stage-manageable. Are you often, bothered and bound in your worship, because you are concerned of what people will say about you? David remembered that it was God who had placed Him at the position he was, he once said; promotion does not come from the east nor from the west but from the Lord (Psalms 75:6).

The children of Israel were warned not to forget the Lord once they got into the land of Canaan and had experienced all the promised blessings.

"Beware that thou forget not the LORD thy God, in not keeping his commandments, and his judgments, and his statutes, which I command thee this day: Lest when thou hast eaten and art full, and hast built goodly houses, and dwelt therein; And when thy herds and thy flocks multiply, and thy silver and thy gold is multiplied, and all that thou hast is multiplied; Then thine heart be lifted up, and thou forget the LORD thy God, which brought thee forth out of the land, of Egypt, from the house, of bondage; Who led thee through that great and terrible wilderness, wherein were fiery serpents, and scorpions, and drought, where there was no water; who brought thee forth water out of the rock, of flint";~(Deuteronomy 8:11-!5)

They were reminded to remember that it is the Lord who empowered them to flourish and be successful in the Promised Land.

"But thou shalt remember the LORD thy God: for It is he that giveth thee power to get wealth, that He may establish his covenant which He swore unto thy fathers, as It is this day" (Deuteronomy 8:18).

David was so careful not to forget where the Lord had taken him. He was merely a shepherd boy at one time. He was the very youngest among all his brethren. He is one whom his family forgot about, when Prophet Samuel came to anoint the one who would be the next king of Israel from among the children of Jesse... He was disregarded, written-off and written-out. Both his father and brothers had disqualified him. It does not surprise me at all that he is the one who said in this Psalm; "Bless the LORD, O my soul: and all that is within me, bless his holy name. Bless the LORD, O my soul, and forget not all his benefits" (Psalms 103:1-2).

He told his wife Michal, who despised him; because of the way he worshipped before the Lord with dancing and played before the Lord. It is children who play; no elderly people play anyhow, but David could humble himself as a child and played like a child before His God. Will you be like a child before your heavenly Father? The only reason David could praise and worship God like this was because

God had promoted him and made him king over Israel in place of Saul, Michal's father.(2 Samuel 6:21).

What matters is doing it as unto the Lord. It was before the Lord, not before man. We dance and worship the Lord, the way we do because we have a story to tell. Do not get offended when we do it in the way that irritates you. Do not be bothered, please excuse me when I do it not in the manner you do it at your church. Please understand me when I choose to worship God not in the traditional way like you do in your church. It maybe you do not know where I am coming from. It maybe you do not know who I was before. It maybe you were not disqualified like I was. It may be that you were not forgotten like I was. It maybe you were not written off like I was. They said I would not amount to anything, but God has favored me, and got me where I am today. I know what He has done in my life. I know where He has taken me from; a place of nothingness to abundance. You may not know it, I was a sinner destined for hell, but he saved and cleansed me with His blood. Do not be surprised when I praise God like I am crazy. When I am shedding tears at times during worship it is because I am touched with what God has done in my life although I did not deserve certain things according to the world. That is why I dare to praise Him so fanatical like no man's business.

It is time to give God the best worship possible. Remember where He picked you from. Consider how He has promoted you. You did not deserve it, but by His grace you are where you are today. Will you purpose in your heart to give Him all the glory that He deserves? Will you worship Him like never before? Will you die to the fear of "what will men say?"

It does not matter where you maybe in the ladder of life right now. Your family and relations might have forgotten you. They might not have wished you well. Men may have disqualified you. They may say you are not the right candidate for that position, for that promotion, for that blessing, but do not worry God is no respecter of persons. He takes things which are regarded as nothing and He makes them into something (I Corinthians 1: 26-29).

Allow me to be a prophet and briefly prophesy into your life right now. You will be taken higher that you or any of your family members ever imagined. God will empower you to become great so that you will be distinguished among your family circles. Some people might have written you off but God is writing you in. Some might have said that you will amount to nothing, but I reverse those negative pronouncements in Jesus name. I now declare in the name of our Lord Jesus Christ that you will amount to all that God has ordained for you to be in this life. I prophesy this scripture 1 Corinthians 1: 26-29. You might have been despised but you shall be esteemed and admired.

Will you believe God for this scripture to be fulfilled in your life?

"For ye see your calling, brethren, how that not many wise men after the flesh, not many mighty, not many noble, are called: But God hath chosen the foolish things of the world to confound the wise; and God hath chosen the weak things of the world to confound the things which are mighty; And base things of the world, and things which are despised, hath God chosen, yea, and things which are not, to bring to naught things that are: that no, flesh should glory in his presence" ~(1 Corinthians 1:26-29).

◇◇◇

CHAPTER 29

FALLING DOWN BEFORE THE THRONE OF GOD

My brethren will you lay down your crowns before God? I would like to draw your attention to something from the scripture passage below. In the following scripture we are shown the picture of how worship is done in heaven:

"And immediately I was in the spirit: and, behold, a throne was set in heaven, and one sat on the throne. And he that sat was to look upon like jasper and a sardine stone: and there was a rainbow round about the throne, in sight like unto an emerald. And round about the throne were four and twenty, , seats: and upon the seats I saw four and twenty, , elders sitting, clothed in white raiment; and they had on their heads crowns of gold. And out of the throne preceded lightings and thundering and voices: and there were seven lamps of fire burning before the throne, which are the seven Spirits of God. And before the throne there was a sea of glass like unto crystal: and in the midst of the throne, and round about the throne, were four beasts full of eyes before and behind. And the first beast was like a lion, and the second beast like a calf, and the third beast had a face as a man, and the fourth beast was like a flying eagle. And the four beasts had each of them six wings about him; and they were full of eyes within: and they rest not day and night, saying, Holy, holy, holy, Lord God Almighty, which was, and is, and is to come. And when those beasts give glory and honor and thanks to him that sat on the throne, who liveth forever and ever, the four and twenty, elders fall down before him that sat on the throne, and worship him that liveth forever and ever, and cast their crowns before the throne, saying, Thou art worthy, O Lord, to receive glory and honor and power: for thou hast created all things, and for thy pleasure they are and were created" ~(Revelation 4:1-11).

In the above scripture the Bible talks about the twenty-four elders as they minister before the Lord. These elders never cease to worship before the throne of God. They are always crying out loud 'Holy, Holy, Holy is the Lord God Almighty, who was and is to come'. These elders are no ordinary men. They are depicted as being high in authority, having their own thrones. The Greek word from which we get the word 'thrones' in this passage is the word 'thronos' and it is the same word used in reference to God's throne, which by implication speaks of power, and authority. Therefore, the twenty-four elders have some kind of authority or high rank in heaven as well.

It is also spoken of the twenty-four elders that they have 'crowns' on their heads. A crown is also-called a diadem, circlet or chaplet as a badge of royalty, a prize like in the public games or a symbol of honor. Thus, these crowns speak of the elders' royalty, and achievements, accomplishments, successes etc

Therefore, in conclusion these elders are not mere men. I can imagine no ordinary man would have a throne in heaven. No mere man would have a crown on his head. This shows us that they are authorities in the Kingdom of God.

However, something unusual happens as they worship God Almighty. They declare His greatness. They do not talk about themselves or their achievement or success. They praise His majesty. They prostrate before the throne of God in worship. In their worship the twenty-four elders reach the extent of leaving where their thrones and fall to the ground.

"Falling to the ground"- ties-up with what happened to John in Revelation 1: 17 'Falling down as though dead'. This seems to be the trend in the Bible. It is prevalent in many places where people encountered the presence of God. When people encountered God's presence they could

224

not just stand, but fell to the ground, overwhelmed by the power of God.

Some of us are too high on our thrones of power, authority, success and influence. In Luke 19: 1-5, the short man named Zacchaeus climbed a sycamore tree in order to see Jesus. He was told to come down if he were to meet the Lord Jesus Christ. In the most African cultures, you cannot talk to the elderly person whilst standing. It is considered disrespectful you stand while talking to an elderly. Respect in such cultures demand that you fall down by kneeling down or sitting down. Will you come down my brother, my sister?

The falling down of the twenty-four elders speak something to us today. When they worship God, they fall down to revere God. They fall down to honor God and declare that He alone is worthy. These twenty-four elders die to self-exaltation, they die to self-esteem, and they die to themselves. These elders know that no matter their positions, they acknowledge that God is above all authority. Falling down speaks of humility; it speaks of giving honor where It is due. God is our sore object of worship. God is the one who deserves all the honor and worship.

The second thing that these elders do is that they prostrate before the throne of God, casting down their crowns to the ground. Since crowns speak of achievements. This then teaches us that no matter how much fame, acclaim, success, you may have. You ought to lay down these things when you come before the throne of the Lord in worship. It is time you acknowledge God in all that you have accomplished. It is time to honor Him with what He has blessed us with, honor God with everything He has enabled you to achieve in this life. Thus, you can come humbly before God and kneel in worship before His throne in all humility. Will you do it now? God is calling you to come before Him in worship. He is above all authority. You can lay your crowns before His throne.

225

You can come and fall before His throne as though dead giving Him all the glory. Never allow your accomplishments to obscure the grace of God. Do not be deceived into thinking that it is your brilliance alone that has made you successful. It is God who gives you all the ability to be successful; whether it be, the intelligence, the wisdom or the energy that enables you to get around daily. Therefore, instead, of crediting yourself with all your achievements, give glory to God. Allow your successes to help you see God's grace at work in your life. And let them act as fuel to propel your worship as an acknowledgement that without Him we can do nothing – for we can have nothing or "receive nothing, except it be given from heaven"(John 3:27).

◇◇◇

CHAPTER 30

THE WORLD IS WAITING FOR THE GLORY

In the book of Chronicles after Solomon dedicated the temple to the Lord, the presence of God descended from heaven and filled the whole house. The Bible records that no priest could stand to minister there in by reason of the intensity of the presence of God. The glory of God filled the house so that no man could stand to conduct all the ceremonial ordinances of worship as they had done traditionally. Oh, how I long for such an encounter; I desire and pray that God will visit us again.

We are living in a time when we need His power more than ever before. If there was ever a moment in history that demands God's presence and glory to be our rear guard, that time is now. The anointing of God is an absolute must if we are to accomplish anything. As we approach the end of times, the battle is going to greatly intensify. It will only take the power from on high to subdue the powers of the devil. It is time we seek God to manifest His glory in these last days. In as much as this will happen by prayer, I strongly believe this will be accelerated by our worship. God is so easily attracted to a people that worship Him. We need to abide in God's very presence in our worship. Many times we tend to walk through God's presence. A peeping, tweeting, mere glancing into God's presence won't do it. A two or three minute prayer will not cut the deal, but a bit more time in His presence is what will attract that heavenly glory, the tangible presence of God.

I can imagine this must be that which also occurred when Peter was so clothed and endued with the Holy Ghost' power, and the glory of God, such that aprons, handkerchiefs that touched the body of Peter brought healing and deliverance upon those that were sick and bound by demons. Even Peter's shadow would radiate

God's glory such that whoever fell under it got healed and delivered. "Insomuch that they brought forth the sick into the streets, and laid them on beds and couches, that at the least the shadow of Peter passing by might overshadow some of them" (Acts 5:15).

This is nothing less than the very glory of God carried in an earthen vessel. This was nothing less than the glory of God at work.

I pray that this will ignite a longing and a desire to experience such manifest glory of God in your life. However, there is a price to be paid. We must be willing to pay the price. It is time we yearn for more of God. Remember, the world lies in great travail waiting for the manifestation of the sons of God. The world is eagerly waiting to see the real power of God in demonstration. This is the power which revolutionizes cities, towns, and nations.

When this glory is experienced it will be an open secret. None will be able to stop this; no one will be able to deny or dispute the authenticity of the miracles and mighty manifestations that will take place. Jesus promised that we as believers will do even greater miracles than He did while He was here on Earth. But the fact remains, we must begin to do something about it. We must make ourselves available before God.

God is looking for nothing else other than our availability and total yieldedness to the Holy Ghost. Is this the desire of your heart as it is mine? I believe the starting point is our desire, the hunger and thirst for God that we will choose to generate. This is what God will satisfy.

The world is tired of churches and preachers that are full of self in their ministry. People are tired of seeing so much performances and acting on the pulpits that is geared to impress the congregation. The world has seen so much of us than of God. It is time that we back off the scene and let God show up. So much of our preaching has yielded few, or very little, if not no result and impact, because we have for a long time done it in our own strength. Paul said in I Corinthians 2;

"And I, brethren, when I came to you, came not with excellency of speech or of wisdom, declaring unto you the testimony of God. "For I determined not to know anything among you, save Jesus Christ, and him crucified" And I was with you in weakness, and in fear, and in much trembling. "And my speech and my preaching were not with enticing words of man's wisdom, but in demonstration of the Spirit and of power"~(1 Corinthians 2:1-3).

Paul did not come with Excellency of man's wisdom, reasoning, and subjective discourse but his preaching was with the demonstration of the power of God "For the kingdom of God is not in word, but in power" ~(1 Corinthians 4:20).

It is time the world knows the God we serve. It is time we stop struggling trying to convince people in our preaching. When this glory comes, it will come with the power that convicts people of sin and ministers the love of God. This is the glory that will cause sinners to repent with brokenness and genuine repentance. It won't be confined to one or few people, but it will touch many people in diverse places. It will no longer be by our power or intellect nor by our might, but by the Holy Ghost (Zechariah 4:7).

The glory draws sinners to the Lord and not to us
You will remember it was the burning bush that drew the attention of Moses while in the wilderness while shepherding the flock of his father in-law, Jethro in Midian. In Exodus 3: 1-4 Moses said, "I will now turn aside to see", that is the attraction.

The same is true when you examine Acts 2:1-4, when the hundred and twenty believers received the promised Holy Spirit in the upper room, it was the smoke, the noise and the tongues of fire which were distributed on each one of the believers which attracted the Jews in Jerusalem and all from around the known world to come and see.

Even these days, we have some Moses', these are people who will only give their attention to the things of God if it is something that baffle their minds, "why is the bush burning, but yet not consumed" For others it will take the wonder that makes them shake their heads in total astonishment, "how can it be that all these 120 people are speaking each in our various languages (tongues) without prior learning of the language"

Naturally man is always seeking some kind of supernatural occurrence, a supernatural manifestation of some kind as I have alluded to earlier. He desires to have an extraordinary spiritual encounter. Jesus said, "The Jews seek a sign while the Greeks seek wisdom". A good percentage of people will be convinced with an intellectual discourse, or reasoning that targets so much their mental faculty. They rationalize the preaching of the word so much. Yet, a great percentage probably over 80% will simply seek after display of power and tangible convincing manifestation of power such as miracles, signs and wonders. When they cannot find it in the church, with men of God, they will seek it in the wrong places. They will look for it outside the church; they end up being ensnared by the spirit of deception and counterfeit. This could be one of the many reasons why some have ended up joining devilish or satanic cults in their pursuit of power and miracles etc

I have heard that Smith Wigglesworth during one of his ministry travels as he walked down the aisle in a train; the power of God was so strong on him that people began falling out of their seats wanting to repent and many people were saved and delivered.

And in another story it is reported that he was sharing a seat with somebody in a train and all over sudden the person next to him came under strong conviction of sin and began to cry in deep repentance. Many would begin to tell him how spiritually unclean they felt. He would then share the gospel and lead them to the Lord in repentance. Smith would minister the Word of God to them without struggles and many people got saved.

This visible presence of the magnificence of God will always bring a difference in the people around us. I am trusting God that we will witness so much of these manifestation of God's glory and power as we decide to make the Lord's presence our habitation. If we purpose to seek and pursue God and stay in worship before the Lord we will experience His glory. If we choose to worship God in our cars, on our beds at night hours, and on the streets, as we do errands, we will definitely walk in His awesome presence.

Let me share with you one last testimony, which took place a couple years back. When I got saved and filled with the Holy Ghost, I would travel with friends from place to place ministering in high schools in our country, Malawi. During one of the meeting at Blantyre Secondary school, the glory of God came as one of my friends ministered the Word of God so that the Holy Ghost came down in His glory in the auditorium where the meeting was taking place. The anointing grew so strong that students who were in their dormitories almost 150-200 meters away started experiencing this glory. Some of them began to cry and repent; they run to the auditorium asking for prayer and help. A number of students got saved delivered and baptized in the Holy Ghost. Oh how, I long for such times when we do not have to struggle to get people saved. I pray that God will send His glory to His church once again in these last days. So much so that even as we walk, sinners will sense the presence of God and get convicted to the point that their heart will melt before us and we can lead them to Christ. I believe this will be our portion if we can get before God with a renewed zeal and hunger for more of God. Will you say with me this prayer to the Lord, "I need more of you Lord in my life, in my church, in my nation?" Will you ask the Lord to visit you again, and rain down His glory you we worship Him?

We are living in a time of the fulfillment of prophecy, a time which was prophesied about that the glory of the latter house shall be greater than the former. The splendor of latter shall exceed that of the former house in its strength.

◇◇◇

CHAPTER 31

HOW TO BRING THE ARK OF THE PRESENCE OF GOD?

The Ark of the Covenant made a difference in the life and family of Obededom the Gittite as we have already seen in some of the preceding chapters. The Bible records that his house and all that pertained to Him were greatly blessed by God. This was not a small blessing, to the magnitude that the news got the attention of King David. Obededom was undeniably, irresistibly blessed so that David took notice of it. And he said, "I will now arise and bring back the Ark" which he was scared of three months prior when he first attempted to bring it to Jerusalem.

We have been without the tangible manifest presence of God for so long; we have suffered unnecessarily as a result of neglecting the Lord's presence. We have strived to make things happen, to get results. Many have not experienced peace and joy; – lives have been empty without any sense of fulfillment while families have become dysfunctional. It is all because of leaving the Ark of the Lord's Covenant out of the family life. But it is time to bring the presence of God back into our homes; it is time to summon the presence of God back to where it belongs, our lives, the temple of God's Spirit. Let us now consider how to bring this Ark of God's presence.

Let us bring the Ark of God's presence

As we endeavor and purpose to pursue the presence of God, you will recall that the Ark of the Covenant represented the very presence of God. It was a reminder of God's everlasting covenant with the children of Israel. Whenever they looked at the Ark, it assured them of God being with them as His people. Whenever the Ark was in their midst it was deemed as though God was there physically present among His people. The Ark was held in highest regard and respect. It was treated with honor.

Not everyone was allowed to carry this Ark except the ones who were ordained and appointed to do that work. "Then David said none ought to carry the ark of God but the Levites: for them hath the LORD chosen to carry the ark of God, and to minister unto him forever" ~(1 Chronicles 15:2).

The people who were so appointed were the Levites. They were charged with this responsibility of carrying the Ark. If we are to experience the power of His presence we need to take our rightful position in the Lord. Let us look at how they actually brought the Ark to Jerusalem the City of David:

"And it was told king David, saying, The LORD hath blessed the house of Obed-edom, and all that pertaineth unto him, , because of the ark of God. So David went and brought up the ark of God from the house, of Obed-edom into the city of David with gladness. And it was so, that when they that bore the ark of the LORD had gone six paces, he sacrificed oxen and fatlings. And David danced before the LORD with all his might; and David was girded with a linen Ephod. "So David and all the house of Israel brought up the ark of the LORD with shouting, and with the sound of the trumpet""~(2 Samuel 6:12-15).

The Levites were not to have an inheritance among their brethren by the command of the Lord, the Lord was to be their portion, and He was to be their inheritance. All the other tribes were to do their various works such as fighting in the army of Israel as soldiers, farming, animal husbandry, and all manner of work and bring their produce and their increase to the house of the LORD in a form of sacrifices and offerings. Therefore, the sore responsibility of the Levites was priesthood which included carrying the Ark of God's Presence.

234

My dear friend, understand that every child of God will face battlefront of challenges, problems; difficulties. At one point the nation of Judah under King Jehoshaphat was surrounded by the enemies who looked stronger and had out-numbered them, so that defeat was eminent. See the story in 2 Chronicles 20:1-2.

You may feel like you are surrounded all around by problems and challenges. It is like battles of life are raging against you all around. I know "many are the afflictions of the righteous: but the LORD delivereth him out of them all...."(Psalms 34:19).

When you purpose to worship the Lord, He will grant you deliverance in the midst of your troubles. The Lord will bring you through it. Know this my friend, if the Lord has brought you to it, He will bring you through it.

"Ye shall not need to fight in this battle: set yourselves, stand ye still, and see the salvation of the LORD with you, O Judah and Jerusalem: fear not, nor be dismayed; tomorrow go out against them: for the LORD will be with you" ~ (2 Chronicles 20:17).

Let the others do the fighting in trying to make things happen and as they try to achieve certain things for themselves. The Levites were not called to fight their own battles, let alone provide for themselves for their own needs, because the Lord was their portion. In the new covenant we are the royal priesthood (1 Peter 2: 9), with a promise from our Lord Jesus, "But seek ye first the kingdom of God, and his righteousness; and all these things shall be added unto you"(Matthew 6:33).

If you choose to be true to your Levitical priesthood in the new covenant, by being the Ark bearer, a worshipper, the one who brings the presence of God down through worship, you will experience sweat-less victories. All these things shall indeed be added unto you. You will not need to fight in this battle; you will need just to take your position of praising and worshipping the master, bearing the Ark of

235

the Lord's Covenant, the presence of God. The Lord God Almighty will fight for you. The nice thing with having the Lord fight for you is that you are assured of the victory – you know in advance that you are fighting an already won battle.

You see the natural mind cannot conceive this because it does not make sense in the natural that one can win a battle by singing or worshipping God. The world, even your fellow brothers and sisters may not understand you when you worship in the midst of your pain, or opposition. It does not make sense to believe God that He can meet your financial need in a failing economy by merely worshipping Him. Others may mock you like Michal did her husband David when he worshipped the Lord with dancing shamelessly before the whole nation of Israel.

The Lord granted victory to Jehoshaphat king of Judah by being sensitive to the Spirit of God, appointing singers and worshippers: the Levites who bearers the Ark of covenant. All they had to do was to take their positions and see the deliverance of the Lord.

And when he had consulted with the people, he appointed singers unto the LORD, and that should praise the beauty of holiness, as they went out before the army, and to say, Praise the LORD; for his mercy endureth forever. And when they began to sing and to praise, the LORD set ambushments against the children of Ammon, Moab, and mount Seir, which were come against Judah; and they were smitten"~(2 Chronicles 20:21-22).

Be assured that victory will be granted to you; your deliverance is on the way. Our enemies are defeated not with much strife. You will simply collect the spoils after the war; you will just get the benefits from the Lord. All you have to do is take your position. This position is the position of bearing the Ark; bringing the presence of God down and carrying His presence, being a worshipper. This is our position where Christ has already placed us. (1 Peter 2:9).

I remember the other day as I was ministering at one of the worship meeting in Blantyre, Malawi, Africa, on the subject 'the power of worship'. I shared with the people that some sickness, demons will go easily by the power of God's presence as we worship. Three people had come into this meeting sick, and I did not know it. But at the end of my preaching I asked everyone to put into practice the word they had just heard. We began to sing and worship the Lord. Everyone went into serious worship before the Lord, forgetting whatever each one was going through. The Lord moved in our midst so much so that God healed the three sick guys instantly without the laying on of hands. They got healed even without rebuking a single demon and they each testified to the power of God. God had confirmed His Word concerning the "Power of Worship" His power comes down among us when we spent time in worship.

The Levitical Priests were to carry the Ark on their shoulders.

It was the Levites who were supposed to assume the role of carrying the Ark of the Covenant from Bethmesheth, or the house of Obed-edom and bring it to Jerusalem not anybody else. Their responsibility was nothing else, but to bring the presence of the Lord to Jerusalem. If ever Jerusalem was destitute, or in dire need of the presence of God it was their fault, and consequently, it was their responsibility to bring it in.

The worship team, worship-leaders are the ones charged with the responsibility of carrying the Ark of the Covenant. They are to bring the presence of God in the house of the Lord in their local assembly whenever they meet for worship.

It is your responsibility as a believer

The Ark of the Lord was to be carried by the priests on their shoulders and not on ox-cart. David and his men made a mistake the first time they attempted to bring the Ark to Jerusalem; it was a mistake in the first place to put the Ark of the Covenant of the Lord on an ox-cart instead of letting the Levites carry it upon their shoulders as ordained by the Lord. Placing the Ark on an ox-cart was a philistine concept, it was a heathen or worldly idea; it was a deviation from the manner it was prescribed in the Bible.

"For, because ye did it not at the first, the LORD our God made a breach upon us, for that we sought him not after the due order" ~(1 Chronicles 15:13).

You see my friend, not every good idea is a godly idea. They had borrowed a worldly idea, they had allowed the world to influence the church or the manner they conducted worship. Many times the spirit of conformity tempts us, where we try to modify our way of doing things in the church to accommodate or attract the unbelievers. It all starts when we compromise in preaching the Word: many preachers tend to dilute the message to people's taste instead of giving it as it is given to them by the Lord. They customize the message to fit certain occasion or classes of people; they do this under the guise of not wanting to offend their members. They want to preach what their members want to hear,. My dear friend, there is no excuse preacher man, this is simply compromise. I know of church services or programs that have once been modified just to accommodate certain so-called dignitaries and politicians attending the service (e.g. taking out the worship and praying in tongues). I was saddened to hear that one of the dignitaries was stunned to observe that there was a change in the program contrary to what he had heard. There was an absence/exclusion of the things he had heard and had expected to see during the service (in particular, how this church worshipped)–he had wanted to experience the way this Pentecostal church worshipped. He had longed to experience that–Unfortunately, it was a missed opportunity. As a church we must remain as crude and true to the way we worship without being apologetic or diffident to the world.

When people of the world come to church they must find us true in the way we know we worship. One thing we must never forget is that people are hungry for the real-deal; they are tired of religion and traditions, they seriously want the authenticity. If it is kneeling down, we should go ahead and do it. If it is worshipping, dancing or prostrating before the Lord we should do it shamelessly without hesitation. Paul said he was not ashamed of the gospel of Jesus Christ (Romans 1:16). Do not change the message in order to appeal or please somebody you view as special when they attend your church service. This is what will impact their lives; the dying world out There is hungry for a true experience or encounter with God. I am surprised when I attend a function organized by non believers to see that they do not modify their program and why should we. We are supposed to set a standard and bring a transformation to the world, not getting conformed to its patterns.

As believers, we are all called to the ministry of priesthood; everyone is a priest in the new covenant. The Church as the body of Christ, we are individually and corporately called to seek the Lord and bring the Ark of God's presence among His people. A "shoulder" speaks of responsibility, just like it is spoken of our Lord Jesus in Isaiah 9: 6 "and the government shall be upon His shoulders" Thus, all the worship teams and their leaders have the role of bringing the presence of God in the churches today. Their role is not to entertain the congregations. They are not to become idols or draw people's attention to themselves through mere performance and display of talent. Their ultimate goal must be to bring the presence of God down as they lead worship in their respective congregation. Our focus must be to draw people into the very presence of God. We are called to personally worship God as individuals, but also to help the people we lead to come to a place where they can personally have a breakthrough in their spirits to worship God intimately.

Consecration is one of the prerequisites

It calls for serious, ample and considered preparation for the worship team and all their leaders and every child of God in order to bear/carry the Ark of God's presence. We are called to a sanctified life. David could only bring the Ark, the presence of God to the place that had been prepared. We ought to get the place of our hearts ready for God's presence. His presence will only come where people are prepared for it. Revival will only come to a nation, a church or a people who are ready and prepared for it. There must be consecrated life as we yield to this call.

"And said unto them, ye are the chief of the fathers of the Levites: sanctify yourselves, both ye and your brethren that ye may bring up the ark of the LORD God of Israel unto the place that I have prepared for it" ~ (1 Chronicles 15:12).

You cannot expect the presence of God upon your life when you live like the World. You cannot live like the world the whole week, and yet expect the glory of God to come on a Sunday morning. There must be a distinction between you as a believer and the unsaved. Choose to be different today. Let the World see the real character of God in your life. Let your light so shine before men. Bear in mind that though we are in the World we are not of this World. So live your life knowing that you are here on earth for the moment.

Ark must be accompanied by joyous jubilation

"Thus, all Israel brought up the ark of the covenant of the LORD with shouting, and with sound of the cornet, and with trumpets, and with cymbals, making a noise with Psalteries and harps" ~ (1 Chronicles 15: 28).

"And David danced before the LORD with all his might; and David was girded with a linen ephod. So David and all the house of Israel brought up the ark of the LORD with shouting, and with the sound of the trumpet" ~ (2 Samuel 6:14-15).

As we purpose to bring the presence of God down, it will require us to forget ourselves. David danced with all his might before all Israel. We must be willing to be undignified, dance the best you know how. The presence of God will descend when we determine to pursue His presence with dancing, shouting, and jubilation.

The Ark of the Covenant was brought with all manner of sound instruments, cymbals, cornet, and harps with much noise. The only place where quietness is the norm is a cemetery– because the people there are dead. The dead can no longer worship God that is why David is calling us in Psalms 150: 5 "Let everything that hath breath praise the LORD. Praise ye the LORD". The Church is alive and well, that is why there will be holy noise in the Church as we bring down God's presence. The Church is supposed to be a place where people can enjoy, celebrate, and be glad.

Learn to enjoy the presence of God. Celebrate the goodness of the Lord. Like David, was so immersed in worship with dancing that he literally forgot himself and just humbled himself before God with shouting and dancing: "And David danced before the LORD with all his might; and David was girded with a linen ephod. So David and all the house of Israel brought up the ark of the LORD with shouting, and with the sound of the trumpet" (2 Samuel 6:14-15).

Please note that David in Verse 12b of the same chapter says, "So David went and brought up the ark of God from the house of Obed-edom into the city of David with gladness". David worshipped God with gladness. The Ark of God's covenant will not be brought with groom, lemon juice baptized faces, but a joyous and jubilant praising body of believers.

David is also the man who also said, "I was glad when they said unto me come let us go to the house of the Lord" (Psalms 122:1). He was excited about attending Church because he knew in the presence of God there is fullness of joy and at His right hand there are pleasures for forevermore. I believe Church must be exciting. It is sad that at times we have made Church so boring that people are no longer excited about Church. I am sorry to say that as believers, we have failed to represent the Kingdom of God well.

We have praised God like we were at a funeral service; this is why unbelievers do not want to have anything to do with Church. We have portrayed Church as boring, unexciting and rigid. When I look at the way many believers behave, if I were unsaved I would not have no interest in such dry mechanical, unexciting, dull praise.

However, many people will certainly try to despise you as you purpose to bring the presence of God. They may mock you in the way you sing, dance or worship before the Lord. David's own wife despised him:

"And as the ark of the LORD came into the city of David, Michal Saul's daughter looked through a window, and saw King David leaping and dancing before the LORD; and she despised him in her heart. And they brought in the ark of the LORD, and set it in his place, in the midst of the tabernacle that David had pitched for it: and David offered burnt offerings and peace offerings before the LORD...... Then David returned to bless his household. And Michal the daughter of Saul came out to meet David, and said, How glorious was the king of Israel today, who uncovered himself today in the eyes of the handmaids of his servants, as one of the vain fellows shamelessly uncovered himself.(2 Samuel 6:16-20).

But the consolation and your courage must come from the fact that it is not unto man that you are dancing unto, but it is unto the Lord. I have always told myself never to be ashamed when it comes to dancing for the Lord. I am not bothered by what people will say about the way I sing or worship in the presence of God. All I care about is pleasing the master. Who is man? No wonder David also said, who is man and whom shall I fear.

Remember the Children of Israel were commanded by God, never to forget the where the Lord and taken them – from the house of bondage, and that it was Him who gave them the power to make wealth. David never forgot everything the Lord had done in his life. (Psalms 103:1-2). David had every reason to worship, dance and shout for the Lord. He told his wife:

"And David said unto Michal, It was before the LORD, which chose me before thy father, and before all, his house, to appoint me ruler over the people of the LORD, over Israel: Therefore, will I play before the LORD. And I will yet, be more vile than thus, and will be base in mine own sight: and of the maidservants which thou hast spoken of, of them shall I be had in honor. Therefore, Michal the daughter of Saul had no child unto the day of her death"~ (2 Samuel 6:21-23).

It is very dangerous to laugh or make fun of men of God. If you cannot or do not understand something about a servant of God, it is better to approach them with humility and ask them. Be not arrogant, but rather open-minded to learn, regardless of your status or position, whether you are a leader or a member of the Church. You may have great background, but your story maybe different with someone

243

else's, do not despise anybody, because you do not know where they have been or where they are coming from. You do not have a clue about the Lord's dealings with the one you maybe despising, or unjustly criticizing.

People that worship God are not simple people, although they may not possess a special look at times. You do not want to heap flaming coals upon your head due to sloppy talk about servants of God; because you may pick a curse upon yourself such as barrenness, stagnation, lack of productivity in life pursuits, unanswered prayers (closed heaven), sickness and even death.

◇◇◇

CHAPTER 32

GIVING: THE NEGLECTED PART OF WORSHIP

People would like to worship God without touching their pockets. You can talk to them about everything and anything else but their money. One preacher once said it is as if some believers during baptism took out their wallets and held them high above the water saying "you may baptize me, deep me in water, except my wallet". They behave as if they accepted Jesus as their Savoir and made Him Lord of their lives except their pockets.

Worship does not begin until we have known that giving is part of our worship to God. You will never claim to be a true worshipper, or one who fears God, if you cannot learn to live a life of sacrifice and offerings. Every man who feared God was a man of sacrifice and offerings.

The Bible talks about a Centurion in the book of Acts 10: 2, "a devout man and one that feared God with his entire house, which gave much alms to the people, and prayed to God always"

Our sacrifices and offerings speak volumes of how much we love the Lord. It is not sufficient to tell someone that you love them. Our love must be accompanied by demonstrable actions. Likewise, we cannot claim to love God in worship and not give into His Kingdom. If we love God, we will also love our fellow man and share with them of our substance.

And if we love God we will be willing to give into the Kingdom for the furtherance of the gospel supporting those ministries which are reaching the world for Jesus Christ. This is apart from the regular tithes and offerings you make to your local church. Your tithe strictly belongs to your local church, where you belong, where you are fed the word of God— Let me emphasize this that you cannot give your tithe to a ministry on TV other than your home church.

You can give to other ministries beyond the parameters of your church, as long as they preach the full gospel of Jesus Christ, the truth of the uncompromising Word of God. As children of God we must mature into sonship where we broaden our horizon with a kingdom-minded outlook. This is where you are prepared to give to people that may never know you or speak about your giving. You give not to receive praise from men, but your giving is unto the Lord so that He who sees in secret may reward you openly. And also know that when you give, a fruit will be credited to your heavenly account.

When David was bringing the Ark of the presence of God into the city of David, he had to make numerous and countless offering and sacrifices. The priest who bore the Ark moved six paces he sacrificed oxen and fatling. I cannot imagine how long this whole trip took for them to get to Jerusalem. Thus, it teaches us to be patient and make time for God- we need to be patient when we are before God; they did not rush through His presence. God wants us to honor Him with our substance. This is another form of worship when we honor Him with all he has blessed us with.

The other side of worship is where you honor the Lord with your giving. When you give to God, you are honoring the Lord, with your substance—it is worship to the Lord as the scripture say, "Honor the LORD with thy substance, and with the first fruits of all thine increase:" (Proverbs 3:9).

In this scripture the word for honor is the same as the one translated to "glorify" Thus our giving to Lord is as good as saying to the Lord be glorified".

I believe our personal devotion and commitment to the Lord is not complete until we learn to honor the Lord with our substance. This includes our tithes and offerings (Malachi 3: 8-10).

Our worship is incomplete unless we compliment our dancing, shouting, falling down and singing with giving to the Lord. In the book of 2 Samuel 6, David did not just dance, shout or sing, but he offered sacrifices in worship to the Lord as they brought the Ark to the city of David. Their jubilation and dancing before the Ark of the Lord's Covenant, the Ark of God's presence was as good as coming before God. You will remember that the Ark represented the presence of God himself, but also remember it is written you shall not appear before the Lord your God empty handed. Here their dances did not replace the requirement for them to offer sacrifices to God as part of their worship. Offering and sacrifices are an integral part of worship.

"Thou shalt keep the feast of unleavened bread:~(thou shalt eat unleavened bread seven days, as I commanded thee, in the time appointed of the month Abib; for in it thou camest out from Egypt: and none shall appear before me empty"~ (Exodus 23:15).

The Language of our offerings

When we come before the Lord with an offering, it is a representative expression of our hearts to Him. How we give is a reflection of our gratitude to the Lord. It is an acknowledgement that all we possess comes from Him. In fact, we are saying to the Lord "what do we have that you have not given us?" We are declaring the preeminence of our Lord in our lives. Our offerings have a voice. They speak to God on our behalf. My friend, bear in mind that when we are passing through certain challenging times, it may be financially or things do not seem to be working out in your favor, these offerings will appear on your behalf before the throne of God's mercy as a memorial. They will plead for your cause; they will say to God, remember his or her faithful giving.

There are times in life when it becomes very difficult for one to pray; your heart may be dealing with depressing stuff to extent that it becomes difficult to open your mouth in prayer to God, your offerings are always before the Lord, they will speak on your behalf (Acts 10: 25-35).

Our offerings also speak denotatively things such as, "Lord you are number one in my life". Giving is a declaration of the Lordship of Jesus as master over our lives including our finances.

Many believers have accepted Jesus as Savior but have not allowed Him to be the Lord over their finances. This is why it is so hard for them to give sacrificially beyond their casual or usual offering. When the Holy Spirit speaks to them to give an amount that they have never given before and it is a big amount, they usually hear another voice saying a different thing. The one voice says, "give it" the other it says," No do not give that amount is too big– you have never given such a huge amount before" This believer usually ascribes those spirit-inspired thoughts to his own mind. The contrary voice discouraging you from giving more is the devil's voice; because the devil knows the only way to keep you struggling financially is by stopping you from giving extraordinary to the Lord. To keep you away from your financial freedom, the devil will discourage you from giving into God's Kingdom. He will do everything possible to convince you that it is not the Lord leading or speaking to you to give beyond the normal. The devil knows the only way to keep you in poverty is to stop you from giving to God sacrificially. The devil knows if he can keep you giving an ordinary offering, he will keep you from receiving an extraordinary blessing. I would say to you, if you hear two voices or thoughts crossing your mind whenever you are about to give an offering, one voice says give $50 and the other says $100, know for sure the one which says a small amount is of the devil, and the one for a bigger one is from the Lord. God does not need our money for His sustenance; it is us who needs His blessings which come when we give to Him. Financial prosperity does not come, because we are praying and fasting a lot, but because we are giving into the Kingdom of God. There is no receiving without giving first.

"Give and it shall be given unto you, good measure, pressed down, and shaken together, and running over, shall men give into your bosom. For with the same measure that ye mete withal it shall be measured to you again"~Luke 6:38

We like to be on the receiving end all the time. We feel blessed when somebody places something in our hands. We even testify of how much the Lord has blessed us. But we never testify that I have been more blessed to give to the Lord. The Bible says, "It is more blessed to give than to receive" (Acts 20:35b).

When the Bible says, give and it shall come back to you. It carries a notion that receiving never precedes giving. The instruction is...give... and the result is that it shall be given back to you... good measure etc

Dear friend, notice that there is a period (.) after the word GIVE. This signifies a point of rest. After you have given rest in the Lord, wait and expect the coming back to you in a good measure... pressed down and shaken together to follow...'

You must believe that God takes pleasure in the prosperity of the saints. He wants us all to flourish in this life not when we get to heaven someday. "Let them shout for joy, and be glad, that favor my righteous cause: yea, let them say continually, let the LORD be magnified, which hath pleasure in the prosperity of his servant" (Psalms 35:27).

God is interested in our complete prosperity which is not just limited to money, but includes good health, wholeness, and peace. This is also one of the reasons Jesus had to die on the cross. He became poor on that cross–He was stripped off of everything; His clothes were taken away from Him by the soldiers who casted lots for them. He was a real example of poverty so that we through His poverty must become rich. "For ye know the grace of our Lord Jesus Christ, that, though he was rich, yet for your sakes He became poor, that ye through His poverty might be rich" (2 Corinthians 8:9).

I believe God wants us blessed beyond measure which also requires a giving that is comparable to the magnitude of the desired harvest. Remember the Bible says with the same measure it shall be measured back to you. The Word of God in 2 Corinthians 9:6 "But this I say, He which soweth sparingly shall reap also sparingly; and he which soweth bountifully shall reap also bountifully"

Here's a principle –our giving will call a corresponding harvest. It is as good as conventional farming; if you want big harvest you make sure you cultivate a reasonable size of the farm.

God is an all sufficient God. He is only offering us an opportunity to partner with Him and be shareholders, co-laborers together with God, so we can be partakers of the heavenly reward. Those who went to war with David received the same share of the spoil as those who were left behind at home watching over the city. You may not go into the mission field yourself but your finances can represent you before God when you support those who are in the mission field touching nations with the gospel of the Kingdom.

I am not talking about the myopic type of giving which is so limited to your local church, but an outward looking which embraces the kingdom concept. I realize there are many Christians that are so narrow-minded that all they think of is their own church. Even some pastors cannot encourage their members to mature and be kingdom

250

purpose-driven believers, to give beyond the four walls of their church building, to sow in other ministries which are working out there in the mission field. Be reminded that we are not here to build our own small kingdoms. We are not here to build notoriety for ourselves, but rather to build the kingdom of God. It is time to think about the Kingdom at large.

At the same time let me point out that I am not talking about tithes here. Other preachers will pray for people and tell them when God has blessed you, bring a tithe to us this is unscriptural. Tithes belong to your local church, the home church; where you belong as a member so that there may be food in that house for the pastors who do not have an inheritance outside of the ministry just like the Levites. However, after you have been blessed indeed and have given your tithe at your local church, you can then freely bless other ministers or ministries beyond your church walls.

> It is easy to give out of the abundance, but it is rather difficult to give out of your living, your very last, the thing you consider your life-saver...

When you come before the Lord with an offering, you are saying to God, I cease to trust in my own strength or money, but I choose to place faith in your divine providence. This may mean giving the very last penny you have. It may well look like the widow with the two little mites (coins). God sees and knows how much we have even in our bank accounts. The size of your offering is measured by how much you are left with after you have given. The amount you give is only a representative of what you have. It is easy to give out of the abundance, but it is rather difficult to give out of your living, your very last, the thing you consider to be your life-saver...or survival kit. I am talking about the giving that

251

goes out to God as your life; where you even feel your heart going with it as you give.

David only wanted to give God something that was of worth, something which meant something to him. David said I will not offer to God an offering that costs me nothing.

"And King David said to Ornan, Nay; but I will verily buy it for the full price: for I will not take that which is thine for the LORD, nor offer burnt offerings without cost" ~ (1 Chronicles 21:24).

Sacrifice is a giving that costs you something. An offering which goes with your heart, where you actually, feel it, you feel it go literally... it goes with some pain, yet you still give it in reverence, obedience and honor to God. There have been times when I have given without feeling anything at all. It happens that the moment the offering is dropped in the offering basket, I usually forget about it. It is like nothing ever happened. This kind of offering is so usual, casual and so ordinary. This kind of ordinary, business as usual type of offering does not carry that element of sacrifice with it. It is not a sacrifice.

But a sacrifice speaks of worship. In the Old Testament the greatest form and part of worship to God was in sacrifices of choicest animals. I believe this was never easy to most them then. And it is no different today, to part away with something that you value so much. Sacrifice speaks of forfeiture and letting go of something. A sacrifice is an offering which is not easily forgotten by the giver as well as the receiver. I strongly believe God never forgets such a sacrifice. I am deeply persuaded that God never forgets such an offering because He sees the heart and everything that accompanies the gift. It is an offering which calls for a recording in the annals of remembrance in heaven.

The amount you give is a direct representative of everything that you have. It also points to how much you have left behind. That offering might appear small in amount to the human eye, but it may be a different case in God's eyes. Therefore, we need to learn to give in proportion to how the Lord has blessed us. That is why no church leader or preacher is to define how much you ought to give when you come to church. You are the one to decide the amount you give to God because your pastor may not know how much you have, except He who gives you the seed.

The offering given in faith is an act of worship

Faith speaks of our dependence and reliance upon God. Our faith speaks and declares of the greatness of our God.

Did you know that our faith is as good as worship before God? Faith speaks of our dependence and reliance upon God. Our faith speaks and declares the greatness of our God. Thus, an offering given in faith is an act of worship. Sacrifices made in faith will definitely speak for us before God of how much we love and depend on Him. In effect, we are saying, 'Lord this money means nothing to me, but you are everything to me'. You are saying, 'Lord I value you more than the money I possess'. It is an acknowledgement that God is our source. What our offering is saying for us to God is, Lord, what do we have that you have not given? We are saying to God, all we possess is already yours. It is an acknowledgement that we are only God's stewards over His trust.

In the Old Testament, many people whenever they wanted to appear before God or whenever they met God, they would make haste to bring an offering to God. They understood the power of sacrifice. They could even restrain the angel of the Lord from leaving them until he had accepted an offering from their hands. Let us consider some of these people who had visitations from the Lord:

253

It is recorded about Manoah: "And Manoah said unto the angel of the LORD, I pray thee, Let us detain thee, until we shall have made ready a kid for thee and the angel of the LORD said unto Manoah, though thou detain me, I will not eat of thy Bread: and if thou wilt offer a burnt offering, thou must offer it unto the LORD. For Manoah knew not that he was an angel of the LORD" (Judges 13:15-16).

Another person is Abraham. It is written that when he was visited by three angels from God to confirm God's promise, he constrained them to wait for a meal offering: "And said, My Lord, if now I have found favor in thy sight, pass not away, I pray thee, from, thy servant: let a little water, I pray you, be fetched, and wash your feet, and rest yourselves under the tree: And I will fetch a morsel of bread, and comfort ye your hearts; after that ye shall pass on: for Therefore, are ye come to your servant. And they said, so do, as thou hast said. And Abraham hastened into the tent unto Sarah, and said, make ready quickly three measures of fine meal, knead it, and make cakes upon the Earth" (Genesis 18:3-6).

If we are to bring the ark of God's presence through worship, we must learn from biblical patterns. We must learn to do it in the manner it was done in the Bible days. If you want to experience the results which the people in the Bible experienced, we must do what these people did. In bringing the ark of God's presence, we can learn from them, "And it was so, that when they that bore the ark of the LORD had gone six paces, he sacrificed oxen and fatlings" (2 Samuel 6:13). Also 1Chronicles 15:26) says, "And it came to pass, when God helped the Levites that bore the ark of the covenant of the LORD, that they offered seven bullocks and seven rams"

Their worship was accompanied by massive sacrifices. We need to make certain sacrifices if we are to bring the presence of God down through praise and worship. We must sacrifice our time; night rests in order to spend a night in prayer in His presence. Sacrifice of your very resources for the Lord. Make sacrifices for the sake of the Kingdom. Give as a way of worship; you can worship God with everything He has blessed you with.

Be willing to go that extra mile, do not worry about what people will say, others will criticize, or even laugh and make fun of you claiming you are overdoing it. They will brand you as crazy. But do not spare do not listen to any discouraging words as they are unleashed against you. Others may even call you fanatic but its best to get fanatical for the Lord than for the devil.

You can purpose to worship God with your resources. When we honor God with our substance, He has promised to bless us so that our barns will be filled with plenty. Our storage houses will overflow with His blessings so that there will not be room enough to contain it. We will be blessed in a big way that these blessings will overtake us. When you stand up to testify, just before you finish saying one testimony another one will be coming your way. You will have one testimony upon another; your mouth will overflow with praise as a result.

Do not hold back in being a blessing to the work of God and other nations. These sacrifices of worship through your giving shall surely stand before the Lord as a memorial which will cause God never to watch you go without. Even before you pray, the Lord will have already taken care of your need.

Giving is the highest form of praise. So let your offering rise up before the Lord and speak on your behalf. They will speak of your love and gratitude to the Lord for all His bountifulness. You can purpose to worship the Lord with your resources no matter how small they may be. Your offering will summon God's blessing and presence into your life and family.

◇◇◇

Conclusion

Are you willing to pay the price?

Remember you are called for intimacy with your creator; this is your primary calling. Serve Him out of your intimate relationship with Him. Dare to lift up a song of praise, a new song in the midst of your difficulty. Hunger and thirst for more of God in your in life, rekindle that zeal for worship, seek Him.

Are you willing to pay the price? Be prepared; deal with anything that can stand in the way of your worship to God. Deal with all sin, unforgiveness and resentment, so you can be prepared to carry and experience the manifest presence of God. Be willing to do whatever it takes to summon His presence into your life, make sacrifices of your time and resources, fast and pray, practice walking or abiding in continual worship in His presence daily. Do not wait for Sunday, open your mouth and worship Him even as you drive, clean the dishes, as lay down in your bed or whatever you may be doing. He is calling you to enter into a more personal, intimate relationship with Him and experience the power of His presence.

◇◇◇

NOW That you KNOW what it takes to Experience the Power of God's Presence and you have the hunger for the more of God, it is time for you to get **EMPOWERED TO SUCCEED:** *a biblical perspective on success.*

In this New Book, Harry takes you through a powerful, heart throbbing, introspective that touches the core of your motives. He speaks about purpose of wealth and what success really is from a biblical perspective. He highlights some of the enduring, self-evident biblical principle keys to success.

He also encourages you to tap into **the limitless power of God for your success; everything** that you will ever need is already provided!!

Get empowered, and succeed **GOD'S WAY.**

Exson ✓ Publishing

Exson Books *the Voice in Word, Impacting Lives*

Get your copy today at www.harrymuyenza.com
or at these and other online stores

And anywhere books are sold

ABOUT THE AUTHOR

Harry Muyenza is a pastor, author, publisher, entrepreneur, and a leader among leaders. He has a calling to be part of end time harvesters, to equip, train, inspire and raise-up leaders who can fulfill their destiny and impact the world. He currently serves as the Senior Pastor of Living Waters Global Church in Mishawaka, Indiana.

He has successfully worked in the corporate world, where he held various senior management positions. He is a graduate of Wings of Eagle International Bible College. Among other qualifications he also holds a Bachelor of Arts Degree in Multidisciplinary Studies (BA DMS) from Siena Heights University, Michigan. Harry is also the founder and President of World Impact for Christ International and Exson Publishing Co.

His ministry has seen him travel to a number of nations. He has been involved in the youth and music ministry, worked with other Christian Organizations among them, The Scripture Union, Student Christian Organization of Malawi, Christ for All Nations(Cfan)- Malawi Crusades, Chapel-Malawi, Dunamis -Norway, His Hands Extended Ministry -USA and Living Waters Global Ministries, Waters of Life Churches International, and Divine Grace Ministries International, in Malawi, United States and South Africa respectively.

He is passionate for souls, desires to see lives saved, transformed, blessed and prepared for the second coming of Lord Jesus Christ. He and his wife, Budile, have two children and they make their home in Mishawaka, Indiana.

www.ingramcontent.com/pod-product-compliance
Lightning Source LLC
Chambersburg PA
CBHW071637050426

42443CB00026B/461